THE *FlyPast* BOOK OF THE
P-51
MUSTANG

ROBERT J. RUDHALL

KEY
BOOKS

Above: Lt L M Granger, of the 350th Fighter Squadron, US 8th Air Force, poses with his groundcrew in front of P-51D *Lady Grace* 3rd. (Ken Delve Collection)

Below: The P-51B was the first variant of the North American design fitted with the Rolls Royce Merlin engine. The tried and trusted Merlin transformed the Mustang, making it one of the most effective of all the Allied fighting aircraft of World War Two. (Key Collection)

Key Books Ltd
PO Box 100, Stamford, Lincolnshire, PE9 1XQ
United Kingdom

Telephone: +44 (0) 1780 755131
E-mail: keybooks@keypublishing.com

First published in Great Britain by Key Books Ltd in 2003

ISBN 0-946219-67-2

British Library Cataloguing in Publication Data:
A catalogue record for this book is available from the
British Library

Designed by DAG Publications Ltd
Printed in China by Sun Fung Ltd

CONTENTS

Wearing the 352nd Fighter Group markings of Lt Col William J Halton's *Slender, Tender & Tall*, P-51D 44-74950/NL51DT is operated by Potomac-based Tom Blair. (Key – Duncan Cubitt)

1 THE HISTORY

If the Supermarine Spitfire was the most famous British-designed and built warplane of World War Two, then North American's P-51 Mustang was undoubtedly the best known single-engined fighter to emanate from the United States of America. The Mustang proved itself in combat time and time again, and it was one of the few fighters the Allies possessed which was able to combine long range with excellent fighting manouverability, a rare attribute for an aircraft of its era.

However, the story of how this great American fighter came into being has its roots firmly lodged in Great Britain. During the late 1930s, a period of high expansion for the Royal Air Force and the British aircraft industry, it soon became obvious that the manufacturing base in the UK would not be able to cope with the anticipated demand for existing designs, let alone new ones. Having established an office in New York, USA, the British Purchasing Commission, under the guidance of Sir Henry Self, was busy placing large orders for a variety of

American aircraft types. Included in these were contracts for hundreds of Curtiss P-40s, despite this fighter's known drawbacks. At that time Curtiss was unable to cope with the required production rate, and so the North American Aircraft Company, which at that stage had only produced training aircraft, was asked to undertake licence production of the P-40.

This idea did not go down too well with North American's president, James H Dutch Kindelberger, who already considered the Curtiss design to be outmoded. Instead, Dutch, with the support of his staff at North American, proposed that the company design and build a totally new fighter aircraft from scratch. This radical idea was to ultimately bring forth the world's best overall fighter of World War Two. However, approval for this proposal had to be sought from the US Congress, as at that time the USA was still following an isolationist policy and did not really want to get dragged into a European war.

Above: A trio of North American P-51D Mustangs formate for the camera. The –D model was really the quintessential Allied long-range escort fighter of World War Two and well over 100 airworthy survivors abound throughout the world today. (Key – Duncan Cubitt)

Below: The North American NA-73X, pictured on an early test flight. Note the somewhat shorter upper cowling carburetor intake, the frameless windscreen and the lack of armament. The aerodynamic smoothness of the airframe is readily apparent in this view. (Key Collection)

Left: This illustration of an early Mustang, carrying USAAF markings, also shows off the clean lines of the aircraft. By the time this photograph was taken the short upper cowling carburetor intake had been replace with a longer example, and the front of the cockpit canopy had become framed in order to accommodate the heavier 'bullet-proof' windscreen. (Key Collection)

In February 1940 a delegation from North American, led by Kindleberger and the company's vice-president, Leland Atwood, travelled to London armed with design sketches, which had been drawn up by Raymond H Rice. Accompanying them was chief designer, Edgar Schmued, along with a pair of assistants. The team then presented their 'case' to the British Air Ministry.

The North American drawings showed a low-wing monoplane of exceptionally clean design, fitted with an in-line engine. Square cut wings and tailplane were also featured in the proposal. Closer examination however revealed some innovations, which would certainly give this aircraft an edge over its contemporaries. Most important of these was a laminar flow wing, the aerofoil section of which had been in development by the USA's National Advisory Committee for Aeronautics (NACA) for some time. This low drag 'signature' presented by the laminar flow wing would certainly aid the fighter's performance figures.

Giving the aircraft an in-line liquid-cooled engine was another plus for the design team. Making the frontal area of the aircraft as streamlined as was possible also afforded performance advantages. However, as with all liquid-

North American need not have worried unduly, as approval was indeed forthcoming, but only on the proviso that two examples of the new aircraft would be given to the US Army Air Corps (USAAC) for evaluation, at no cost!

FOURTH OF THE MANY

Undoubtedly the most historic of all surviving Mustang airframes in the world is XP-51 41-038, the fourth example 'off the line'. North American's test pilot Robert Chilton took this aircraft aloft for the first time on May 20, 1941. After completing a series of evaluation flights at Wright Field between August and December, it was flown to Dayton, Ohio in company with 41-039, the second of the XP-51s supplied to the United States Army Air Corps.

After spending some time at Dayton, both of the XP-51s were transferred into the care of the National Advisory Committee for Aeronautics and moved to Langley Field, Virginia, for use as test-bed airframes. When World War Two came to an end 41-038 was flown to Orchard Airport, Illinois, (now better known as Chicago O' Hare Airport), where (with great foresight) the USAAF was gathering together a collection of significant aircraft

for future display in a museum. In early January the Mustang, along with all the other 'museum' aircraft, was transported to the National Air and Space Museum's facility at Silver Hill, Maryland. 41-038 was to spend the next 25 years of its life in storage at this location.

In 1974, as part of a complex trade arrangement, the XP-51 was transferred to the Experimental Aircraft Association's (EAA) Air Museum Foundation and '038 was moved to Hales Corner, Wisconsin (then the main base of the EAA) in the spring of 1975. Just over one year later the Mustang returned to the skies after a painstaking restoration by Darrell Skurich.

Skurich, owner of the warbird restoration company Vintage Aircraft Ltd at Fort Collins, worked wonders on the XP-51, as the aircraft had not fared well during its 25 years of storage at Silver Hill. Major parts of the airframe had been damaged and if that was not

enough to contend with, it was found during the rebuild process that the XP-51 was virtually 'handbuilt', the design of parts and mass construction tooling not having been put into place by North American at that early stage of Mustang production. A lot of North American T-6 Texan/Harvard parts had been utilised and none of the hydraulic components were standardised with later Mustang construction.

A completely new coolant radiator had to be built by a specialist company, as the aircraft's original had not been drained properly during the time the airframe was in storage, and had subsequently suffered irrepairable frost damage. The Allison engine was totally overhauled by John Sandberg's JRS Enterprises company at Minneapolis, during which the opportunity was taken to convert the early-build Allison into a later, much more reliable engine.

Eventually the restoration to flying condition was completed and the airframe was given a coat of Alumigrip silver laquer to simulate 41-038s original bare metal finish. The XP-51 made its first public airshow appearance at the EAA Fly-in and Airshow at Oshkosh in 1976, after which it was only flown on specially selected occasions.

After making several appearances it was decided not to risk flying this significant aircraft any longer and it was permanently grounded and placed in a place of honour inside the EAA's AirVenture Museum at Oshkosh, where it can still be seen today. A fitting retirement for one of America's most famous World War Two aircraft! (Key – Ken Delve)

cooled engines the problem of where to put the coolant radiator was often a thorny one.

When the highly experienced British aircraft designer R J Mitchell laid down plans for the Supermarine Spitfire he placed the radiator underneath one of the aircraft's wings. When on the ground the radiator housing was partially blanked off by one of the undercarriage legs, causing temperature problems while the aircraft was running on the ground. When airborne, with the undercarriage tucked away in the wing, the problem solved itself, but the location of the radiator proved to be troublesome when Spitfires were in combat. All it took was one stray bullet to penetrate the radiator housing and the fighter suffered severe cooling problems. This often led to a forced landing, or worse, the pilot bailed out and the aircraft was lost.

After much consideration the North American engineers decided to place the radiator on the under-fuselage, behind and below the cockpit in order to preserve the aircraft's nose streamlining. While this position dictated the use of considerably more plumbing than one positioned close to the engine, it did have a distinct advantage in that the air passing through the radiator could be expanded, accelerated and ejected through a controllable flap at the rear of the housing. This in turn provided extra propulsion, which more than made up for the drag imposed on the airframe by the radiator.

In terms of armament the North American design originally included four .50 calibre machine guns, or a mixture of two .50s and two .30s. The British Air Ministry found this to be unacceptable and insisted that the fighter's armament should at least be equivalent to that being carried by the Hurricanes and Spitfires currently serving with RAF Fighter Command.

The powerplant was the next area to come under scrutiny. The most powerful in-line engine in the USA during early 1940 was the Allison V-1710. Producing 1,150hp (857.9kW) at 11,800ft (3,596m), this engine was designed to offer its best performance at lower altitudes, which suited what the RAF required of a tactical fighter. With the benefit of hindsight, it was this performance which, after the aircraft had entered service, gave cause for concern and ultimately led to the Mustang being re-engined with the Rolls Royce Merlin.

Just 120 Days!

At the end of a series of meetings both parties agreed on the new aircraft's requirements and a Letter of Intent was followed by a formal contract on May 23, 1940. There was one stipulation, and that was that the prototype

should be completed within 120 days of the formal contract being issued!

This was a tall order for any aircraft company of the period to take on board. For North American it was even more daunting, for up until then it had only been involved in producing training aircraft. Nevertheless the relatively small workforce at Mines Field, near Los Angeles, applied themselves magnificently and defying all the odds pushed the prototype of the new fighter, by now designated as the NA-73X, out of the assembly shed just 117 days after work had originally started. However, the aircraft was still awaiting its engine from Allison, and the wheels and tyres fitted to the airframe had been borrowed from an AT-6 Harvard trainer. That apart it was an incredible feat to say the least!

28 days later the engine arrived and was fully fitted in the aircraft within 24 hours. The brand new North American fighter was ready for testing. October 26, 1940, and the NA-73X stood poised at the end of the runway at Mine Field. Test Pilot Vance Breese opened the throttle and the aircraft sped down the runway on its stable wide-track undercarriage.

After a 20-minute problem-free flight the fighter landed and Breese subsequently carried out three more sorties before handing the test schedule over to North American's test pilot, Paul Balfour.

Above: Mustang I AG346 was the second production P-51 built for the Royal Air Force, but was the first to actually arrive in the UK. Pictured during its initial evaluation period with the RAF in November 1941, it was eventually lost on operations when it was shot down by anti-aircraft fire on August 20, 1944. (Key Collection)

Below: In typical wartime propaganda style, the original company caption on the back of this photograph reads: "Three of North American Aviation's powerful new A-36s, which are dive bomber versions of the company's Mustang design, are shown flying in formation over Southern California. Designed to hit hard and get back safely, the A-36s are the world's fastest dive bombers, with a flying speed in excess of 400 miles per hour". (Key Collection)

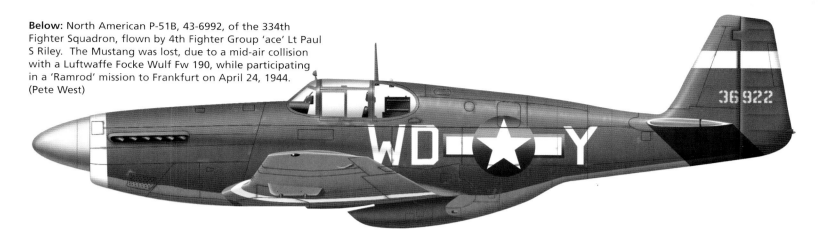

Below: North American P-51B, 43-6992, of the 334th Fighter Squadron, flown by 4th Fighter Group 'ace' Lt Paul S Riley. The Mustang was lost, due to a mid-air collision with a Luftwaffe Focke Wulf Fw 190, while participating in a 'Ramrod' mission to Frankfurt on April 24, 1944. (Pete West)

Below right: Mustang I AM190, an RAF cannon-armed machine, saw service with the Aeroplane and Armament Experimental Establishment, Boscombe Down, Wilts, and also flew operationally with 516 Squadron. It survived the war and was struck off charge on October 31, 1945. This view shows the flat-sided heavily-framed cockpit canopy which gave a somewhat restricted view for the pilot. (Key Collection)

Below: Allison-engined Mustangs had their machine gun armament replaced with four 20mm cannons, which featured removeable fairings. Each gun was provided with 125 rounds and the pilot was also given the choice of firing just two of the cannons (one in each wing) or all four at once. For ease of maintenance, access to the cannons was made simple by the use of just one Dzus fastener in a cover plate on the upper surface of the wing. Note also the small under-fuselage radiator housing, compared to the later P-51D variant. (Key Collection)

During its first flight with Balfour at the controls the NA-73X crashed following an engine failure and forced landing. Severely damaged following the landing in a ploughed field, it was discovered that the engine had stopped due to fuel starvation. The pilot had allowed one fuel tank to run dry and had not changed tanks quickly enough.

The crash of the prototype, through no fault of its own, had thankfully not given cause for the RAF and British Air Ministry to change their minds and cancel the project. Further flight-testing was carried out using the first example (AG345) from the RAF's first order of 320 aircraft. A pair of airframes, designated XP-51 (41-038 and 41-039), actually the fourth and tenth aircraft off the production line, were transferred, as arranged, to the US Army Air Corps for test purposes.

The flight test programme was now in the hands of Robert C Chilton, who had been brought in to replace Balfour. Confidence in the aircraft was shown just a few days after the prototype's accident when word came through from England that the name Mustang had been chosen for the new fighter.

By the autumn of 1941 the second production machine (AG346) had flown successfully and was then shipped over to the UK. The voyage across the Atlantic was an eventful one, as the convoy of ships was attacked by a Luftwaffe Focke Wulf Fw 200 Condor. If the Germans on board the Condor maritime patrol bomber had only guessed that in a few years time North American Mustangs would be driving them out of the skies over Europe, they may have pressed home their attack with more vigour!

Arriving at Liverpool Docks in October the crate containing AG346 was unloaded and taken immediately to Speke Aerodrome, where it was unpacked and assembled in readiness for flight-testing. Pilots who took the Mustang aloft confirmed the aircraft's favourable flying characteristics, which had already been enthusiastically reported by those who had flown the fighter in the USA. During the following weeks Mustangs began to arrive in Britain on a regular basis as production in the USA got into its stride.

A pair of Mustangs, from an early batch that arrived in the UK, were seconded to the Air Fighting Development Unit at RAF Duxford, Cambs, where they were flown in evaluation trials alongside Spitfires and other contemporary types.

Recognised as an effective low-level aircraft, Mustang Is entered service with Army Co-operation Command

Above: FX883, a Merlin-engined Mustang III, one of a batch of 250 delivered between November 1943 and February 1944, not only carries a Royal Air Force serial, but sports American 'star and bar' national markings. Indeed, it was transferred back to the USAAF on December 30, 1943. According to the photograph's wartime caption "The new Mustang was recently described by Major Thomas Hitchcock, Assistant Attaché for Air in London, as the airplane destined to be the world's outstanding fighter plane in 1943". (Key Collection)

Centre: Just ten airframes down the production line, Mustang III FX893 stayed with the RAF and is pictured while on a test flight during its time with the Aeroplane and Armament Experimental Establishment, where it underwent wing-mounted rocket trials. This aircraft has been fitted with a 'Malcolm' blown cockpit canopy, which went a long way in providing better visibility for the pilot. At least now he had an element of rearward vision. FX893 later went on to see service with the RAF in the Middle East. (Key Collection)

Left: Rare wartime colour photo of '49378', a shark-mouth-nosed A-36 Apache dive bomber variant of the Mustang. This well used-looking aircraft saw much operational service with the USAAF's 14th Air Force in China. (US National Archives)

Below: The Royal Air Force's 112 Squadron was well-known for its sharkmouth insignia which adorned its P-40 Kittyhawks. The unit also applied the impressive nose-art to its Mustang IIIs, as illustrated by this view of FB309. (Pete West)

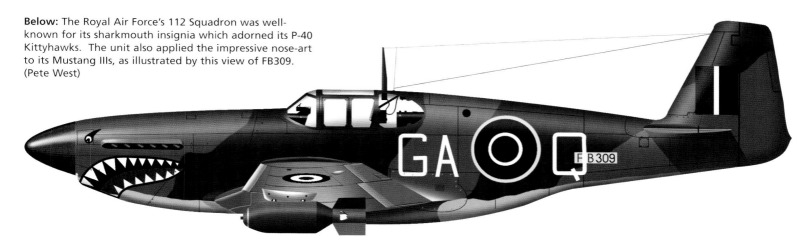

Below right: The P-51B was the first major mark to adopt the Rolls Royce Merlin engine. Licence-built by Packard in the United States, the Merlin transformed the Mustang into the supreme fighting aircraft it would become. Able to hold its own in any dogfight scenario at height, it also gave the aircraft its 'long legs' which enabled it to stay with the formations of Allied bombers all the way to and from the targets in enemy occupied Europe. This shot of 43-12201, taken on a test flight, shows the even-more streamlined nose area, plus the deeper radiator housing, caused by the Merlin needing extra cooling capacity. (Key Collection)

Below: The vast majority of the RAF's Allison-engined Mustang Is were used in the Army Co-operation and low level reconnaissance role. The port for the oblique camera can be seen in the fuselage behind the pilot, where it replaced one of the 'quarter light' Perspex panels. (Key Collection)

(ACC) and flew their first offensive sortie on July 27, 1942. The following month Mustangs were used in support of the ground troops during the ill-fated Dieppe operation. In RAF service the Mustang became the first single-engined UK-based fighter to penetrate airspace beyond the German border. The on-board fuel capacity of 180 US gallons, housed in a pair of self-sealing tanks, gave the fighter a range of up to 1,000 miles (1,609km). Originally some 18 squadrons of Mustang Is were planned for ACC, but the maximum operational units at any one time never exceeded 16.

Mainly operating in the Tactical Reconnaissance role, Mustang pilots were initially instructed to avoid engaging the enemy if at all possible, although Flying Officer Hollis H Hills (an American flying with the RAF), of 414 (RCAF) Squadron, managed to score the first Mustang victory, when he shot down a Focke Wulf Fw 190 over Dieppe on August 19, 1942. At that time Hills was a US citizen, but later in the war joined the US Navy, scoring four more kills while flying Grumman F6F Hellcats in the Pacific.

American Interest

As the British units gained valuable experience with the Mustang, the United States Army Air Force (USAAF) began to take an interest in the aircraft. Two XP-51s had been taken on charge by the USAAF for evaluation purposes during the latter part of 1941. With the USA now firmly involved in World War Two, following the Japanese attack on Pearl Harbor (Dec 7, 1941), the Mustang was looked at again in greater detail. Following extensive tests of the XP-51s, during which engine performance, propeller and gun trials were carried out, it was decided to transfer 57 production P-51 aircraft from the RAF's Mustang IA order to the USAAF, and 55 of these were fitted with cameras to become designated F-6As.

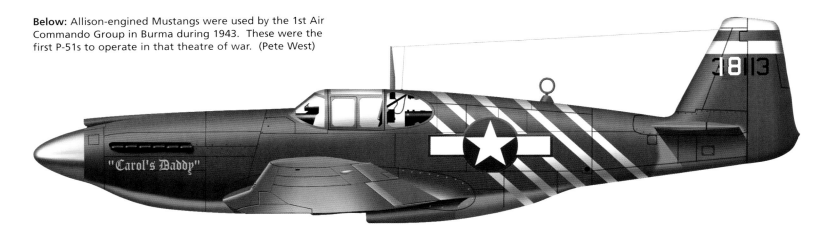

Below: Allison-engined Mustangs were used by the 1st Air Commando Group in Burma during 1943. These were the first P-51s to operate in that theatre of war. (Pete West)

The first of these were dispatched to the USAAF's Photo Reconnaissance School at Colorado Springs. In the meantime North American had put forward a proposal for a ground attack version of the aircraft, to be designated A-36. The variant was officially adopted and the first A-36s started to roll off the production lines in September 1942. This version would also be used for dive-bombing; fitted with dive brakes it was capable of carrying a pair of 500lb bombs, which were attached to wing racks.

Seeing as it would be subjected to extra stresses during this role the airframe was surveyed and a number of modifications were made 'beef up' the structure. The A-36 was also given an uprated engine, which produced more power at low altitude. However, this was not as effective as had been expected, as the A-36 was heavier than a P-51 and the wing bomb racks caused extra drag.

In September 1942 a contract for 1,200 P-51A fighters was issued by the USAAF, initially with the aircraft being allocated the name Apache (although in some theatres of operation it was also called Invader). These names were subsequently dropped in favour of the British name - Mustang

A New Engine

With continued use of the new fighter within the RAF, it was ascertained that, while the aircraft was capable at low level, it swiftly lost performance during high-level operations. It was the un-supercharged Allison engine, which was proving to be the Mustang's achilles heel. A solution had to be found for this fundamental problem if the aircraft was to enjoy a successful military career. Ronald Harker, a test pilot with engine manufacturer Rolls

Centre: Before too long Merlin-engined marks of the Mustang began arriving with the USAAF's 8th Air Force in the UK. 43-12166 is a standard olive drab camouflaged machine, which, when this photograph was taken, had yet to be allocated to an operational unit. (Key Collection)

Bottom: This natural metal-schemed P-51B, 42-106767, served with the 334th Fighter Squadron, 4th Fighter Group, USAAF 8th Air Force. The 4th FG converted from its previous P-47 Thunderbolt mounts to P-51 Mustangs in an amazing 24 hours! One of the great fighter units of World War Two, the 4th included several 'aces' among its pilots, Duane Beeson, Don Blakeslee, Don Gentile, John Godfrey and Ralph Hofer, to name just five. (Key Collection)

Below: The *Verna Q,* a Merlin-engined 'high-back' Mustang, was flown in combat by Major Frank O' Connor of the 354th Fighter Group. (Pete West)

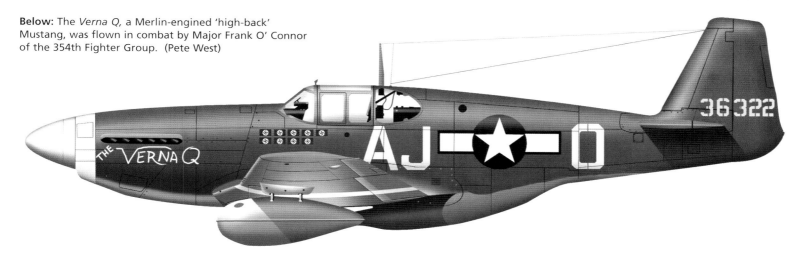

Royce, was invited to fly a Mustang at the Duxford-based Air Fighting Development Unit. After just a short time in the air Harker realised that fitting the Mustang with a Rolls Royce Merlin engine could dramatically transform the fighter's performance characteristics. This transformation could not be carried out on an ad-hoc arrangement, it had to take place with official backing. Lord Hives, Rolls Royce's technical director, was consulted and subsequent calculations for a Merlin-engined Mustang showed that it would immediately have a 70 mph speed advantage over the Allison-equipped variant. A serious improvement indeed!

With this, and other advantageous performance figures to hand, plans were put into action to carry out the conversion process on three RAF airframes, AL963, AL975 and AM121. These three aircraft flew to the Rolls Royce airfield at Hucknall and work began to fit the Merlin into the Mustang's airframe. Conversion work also took place in the USA, where North American Aviation fitted a US Packard-built Merlin into the XP-51B. A sort of unofficial race took place between the engineering teams at Hucknall and those in the USA to see who would be first to complete the task in hand. In the event, Hucknall won by six weeks, when AL975 flew under the power of a

Right: With its squared-off wings and tail area, the early 'high-back' P-51s were sometimes mistaken for Luftwaffe Messerschmitt Bf 109s and therefore, to aid airborne aircraft recognition skills, Mustangs carried white noses and white stripes on the wings and tail surfaces. These cosmetic additions obviously clashed somewhat with the olive drab camouflage carried by the fighters at that period of World War Two. (Key Collection)

Right: P-51B 43-12102 was removed from the production line in the USA and converted into what, in effect, was the prototype P-51D. With its cut down rear fuselage and bubble canopy the –D model Mustang was classed by many who flew and fought in this variant, as the best of all marks of the Mustang. It did have its initial teething problems, in that the aircraft suffered from a lack of directional stability due to the lack of 'high-back' fuselage. This problem was virtually cured when an additional fuselage to fin fillet was fitted on later airframes to emanate from the factories. (Key Collection)

Merlin on October 13, 1942. The American XP-51B took to the air on November 30.

Known as the Mustang III in RAF service and as P-51B in USAAF parlance, the transformation of the fighter was to say the least, stunning! That said, there were some drawbacks caused by the fitting of the Merlin engine. The Allison-powered Mustang was reported to be a pleasant aircraft to fly, its pilots considering it to be almost perfect from an aerodynamic point of view. The Merlin Mustang was a much more demanding aircraft, its more powerful engine and four-blade propeller caused more torque, which in turn, affected directional stability. The aircraft also required a higher number of control adjustments in order to keep it properly trimmed in flight. While it was not as pleasant to fly, the Merlin Mustang's performance and combat potential was unquestionable.

By June 1943 production on the Merlin Mustang was well underway at North American's Inglewood factory. In August of the same year, North American's other facility

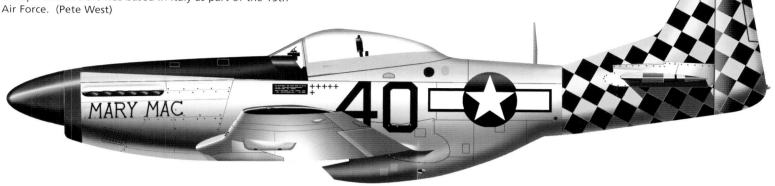

at Dallas, which up until then had been concentrating on other types, was turned over to P-51 production. The first batch of P-51Bs sent to the UK were taken on strength by the 354th Fighter Group, US 9th Air Force, where they would initially be used as a tactical force to support the land armies in the soon-to-come invasion of enemy occupied Europe. The decision to use the fighter for what amounted to be ground-support duties did not go down too well with those who were fighting in the US 8th Air Force. The 8th had been suffering high losses in the daylight raids over Europe and the bombers were in dire need of an escort fighter with the potential of the Merlin-engined P-51.

Likewise the 9th AF was not keen on losing this effective fighting machine but, after a series of negotiations between USAAF policy makers, a compromise was reached in October 1943. The Mustangs of the 9th would support and escort the bombers of the 8th. The 354th FG arrived in the UK during November 1943 and after only two days based at Greenham Common, Berks, started operating out of Boxted Airfield, near Colchester, Essex. During operations with the Mustangs, pilots found that one of the worst aspects of going to war in this aircraft was the less than acceptable visibility from the cockpit.

As a stop-gap solution the British experimented and fitted some of their Mustangs with a bulged Perspex sliding canopy, which had been designed by Malcolm Aircraft Ltd, a company which was producing special cockpit canopies for high altitude Spitfires. This solved the immediate visibility problem and what soon became known as

'Malcolm hoods' were quickly fitted to RAF Mustang IIIs and some USAAF P-51Cs. Those flying the Mustang need not have worried unduly over the visibility problem as an ultimate solution was about to appear on the horizon.

In the USA plans were afoot for a major redesign of the P-51 airframe. In order to solve the view problem, it was decided to cut down the rear fuselage of the fighter and fit a one-piece streamlined bubble canopy. This new P-51D variant would also have a more powerful Packard Merlin and a stronger wing with six 0.5 machine guns. All in all it was a quantum leap forward, even though, surprisingly, the 'D model was marginally slower than the earlier variants! However, of more concern was the P-51D's apparent lack of directional stability. With the cut down rear fuselage to accommodate the bubble canopy a substantial amount of fuselage 'high-back' had been removed, and it was only with the fitting of an extra fuselage to fin fillet that the directional stability problem was brought back to an acceptable level.

With the new mark well into production, just 280 P-51Ds were delivered to the RAF, where they were known as Mustang IVs. The vast majority of the production runs (6,502 built at Inglewood and 1,454 at Dallas) went to the USAAF, where they would be used with great effect in Europe and the Pacific. The fighter's extreme range made it especially ideal for 'long-legged' bomber escort duties and fighter sweeps over the wide-ranging areas of the Pacific.

The first consignments of P-51Ds to arrive in Europe were allocated to group and squadron commanders, who

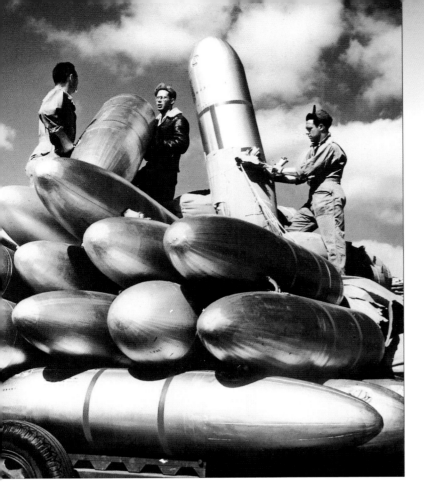

51 fought hard in many other theatres of war, which are often overlooked. During the summer of 1943 a pair of USAAF fighter/bomber groups (FBG), serving in 12 Air Support Command, Northwest African Forces, were equipped with the A-36 variant of the Mustang. Aircraft of the 27th and 86th FBGs took part in operations leading up to the Allied landings on Sicily in 1943. Operating, in the main, against enemy airfields, defensive positions and lines of communication, the A-36s provided sterling service and, after the fall of Sicily, moved on to support operations for the Allied attack on Salerno. It was in this theatre of operations that the aircraft gained the name Invader, for as one pilot of the period put it "we called it the Invader because we seemed to be doing nothing else but invading different countries with it!"

The 31st and 52nd Fighter Groups, which had been equipped with Supermarine Spitfire Vs for the North African campaign, re-equipped with P-51D Mustangs in the Spring of 1944 and subsequently carried out tactical operations with the 12th Air Force. By early 1944 the USAF's heavy bombers were carrying out raids on airfields in the Foggia region, southern Italy. Up until then they had relied on escort fighters such as the P-38 and P-47, which, while effective in their own way, did not have the long range required to keep the bombers covered for the entire mission.

With the arrival of the Mustangs of the 31st Fighter Group in the Spring of that year more potent use of air power could take place. The first 'thrust' for the 31st came on April 21, when it was detailed to provide fighter cover for B-24 Liberators after they had carried out a raid on the oil fields at Ploesti. This operation would later go down as one of the most famous air attacks of World War Two and ranks alongside the RAF's legendary 'Dam Busters' raid carried out by Lancasters in May 1943. While bringing the bombers back home the Mustang pilots engaged enemy fighters and succeeded in shooting down 17 of them. This action earned the group a Distinguished Unit Citation.

1944 also saw a major increase in the use of Mustangs in the Pacific Theatre. The 10th Air Force had been using A-36 and P-51 variants during the latter part of 1943, supporting the American-Chinese advance on Myitkyina, and the F-6 photo recce version was also operating with the

would make better use of the improved visibility aspect. However, before long all but 15 of the USAAF's fighter groups were equipped with the Mustang. All but one of the 8th Air Force's P-47 Thunderbolt groups were eventually changed over to P-51Ds. The Mustang certainly reigned supreme. It was the only Allied fighter capable of escorting bombers all the way on deep penetration raids in which landings were made in Russia or North Africa after taking off from bases in the UK or Italy.

The P-51D had the long legs to accomplish this, while at the same time still being able to hold its own in dogfight scenarios. Time after time the bombers of the 8th Air Force would be escorted by their 'little friends' (as the Mustangs and other types soon became known) out to the targets only to be 'bounced' by enemy fighters. The Mustangs were able to jettison their underwing fuel tanks and offer effective protection to the bomber stream. After the marauding fighters had been beaten off the P-51s resumed their escort duties.

Other Theatres

While it is the European air war that has captured most of the attention in the telling of the Mustang's story, the P-

Below: One of the most distinctive paint schemes to be worn by 8th Air Force Mustangs was this black and white chequerbord set of markings applied to the P-51s of the Duxford, UK-based 78th Fighter Group. P-51D *Contrary Mary* was flown by the 84th Fighter Squadron in August 1945. (Pete West)

Below: Standard clothing for P-51 pilots comprised of a leather flying jacket, with 'Mae West' lifejacket, fur-lined gloves, leather helmet and goggles, plus rubber oxygen/radio mask. While the Mustang's cockpit was relatively roomy, in comparison with other World War Two fighters, by the time the pilot was wearing all this 'apparel' it still made the working area in the cockpit quite cramped! (US National Archives)

8th Photographic Reconnaissance Group in the same area. In March 1944 the P-40-equipped 51st Fighter Group gave up its Warhawks for P-51B and C-model Mustangs and in November the 82nd Reconnaissance Squadron shed its P-40s and replaced them with Mustang F-6Ds.

Following the bloody battle to capture the islands of Iwo Jima, Mustangs of the 15th Fighter Group started arriving at South Field on March 6, 1945. Taking a very short time to establish themselves the fighters were declared operational on March 8 and on March 10 were undertaking patrols over the US Navy carriers, which were then in the process of leaving the area.

Flights of eight Mustangs provided constant cover between the hours of dawn and dusk. Other P-51s carried out strafing missions, shooting up enemy pillboxes, gun emplacements, troop convoys and other facilities. The presence of the Mustangs in the sky greatly boosted the morale of the hard pressed ground troops. Proving time and time again its worth in aerial combat and ground

support operations the P-51 really helped to turn the course of the war in the Pacific. Long range fighter escort was now being provided as a matter of course.

On April 7, 1945, 108 Mustangs of the 8th Fighter Command escorted B-29 Superfortresses of the 73rd Bombardment Wing on a raid against the Nakajima-Musashi factory complex. This was the first time that American land-based fighters had operated over the Japanese home islands. This was undertaken using two 165 US-gallon drop tanks fitted under the wings of the P-51s.

Subsequent operations saw Mustangs flying with six High Velocity Aircraft Rockets (HVAR) fitted underneath the wings, in addition to the drop tanks. This raised the aircraft's operating weight well over its maximum of 12,500lb (5,670kg) and sometimes made the fighter's take off runs protracted and difficult for the pilots. Nevertheless the Mustangs still flew and performed admirably!

A Twin-Engined Mustang

During mid-1943 it became obvious that a new long-range escort fighter was needed to provide extra cover for the B-29 Superfortress bombers in the Pacific theatre. North American Aviation began design work for an aircraft which would meet this criteria. It was a simple idea, join two Mustangs together with a common wing centre section! However, like all simple ideas, it proved to be more complex than was first thought.

Giving the project the designation NA-120, the twin fuselages were basically those from the P-51H variant, but throughout the design process they underwent so many different modifications and changes that they emerged to be almost totally different from the original. Each fuselage was fitted with an individual fully castoring tailwheel, while the main undercarriage legs were attached to the root of the outer wing panels, retracting into the new wing centre section. The wing centre section also housed the standard complement of six 0.50 cal machine guns. This could also be supplemented with a detachable pod containing eight 0.50 cal guns, giving the aircraft a formidable array of firepower.

Three protoypes were requested, two fitted with Packard-built Merlin V-1650 engines (XP-82) and the third (XP-82A) with Allison V-1710s. The latter was built as 'insurance' just in case the British government cancelled the licence, which enabled the Packard company to build the Rolls Royce Merlin. The first of the Merlin-powered machines flew on April 15, 1945, just 16 months after work had started on the project.

Left: This painting by renowned artist Keith Hill, depicts a P-51D of the 353rd Fighter Group somewhat worse for wear after an entanglement with Luftwaffe Messerschmitt Me262 jet fighters. The pilot of the Mustang is shown bailing out of his stricken aircraft. (Keith Hill Studios – www.KeithHillStudios.co.uk)

Left: During World War Two Mustangs appeared in a number of colourful paint schemes, as individual USAAF fighter units established their own identities. One of the most distinctive colour schemes carried by US 8th Air Force P-51s was that of the 78th Fighter Group, based at Duxford, Cambs. The black and white chequerboard nosed P-51Ds could not really be mistaken for any other unit. Initially operating with P-47 Thunderbolts, the 78th came into its own when re-equipped with Mustangs, under the command of Colonel John D Landers. Several of today's preserved airworthy Mustangs carry 78th FG markings, this example (NL51ES) is owned and flown by American airshow pilot Ed Shipley and was caught by the camera at the Hamilton International Airshow, Canada, in June 1998. Its *Big Beautiful Doll* markings reflect those worn by Col Landers' personal P-51D during the war. (Key – Duncan Cubitt)

Left: A mixture of P-51C and P-51Ds of the 8th Air Force's 375th Fighter Squadron, 361st Fighter Group, head out for another deep penetration bomber escort mission around the D-Day period of World War Two. Note the long-range drop tanks, which were jettisoned once enemy fighters were sighted. (Ken Delve Collection)

The Merlins drove propellers which were designed to rotate inwards towards each other. This virtually eliminated the usual torque problems normally associated with piston-engined propeller-driven aircraft. The pilot was housed in the port cockpit, while a co-pilot/navigator sat under the starboard canopy. Only the port cockpit contained a full complement of flight controls and instrumentation, whereas the starboard cockpit featured adequate flight controls and enough instrumentation to enable relief and emergency operation of the aircraft.

If the P-82 was to be used in the ground attack and fighter-bomber role the starboard cockpit could be removed and faired over. The outer wing panels were modified, in that the armament was removed and a pair of underwing pylons were fitted to enable the aircraft to carry either two external fuel tanks or 1,000lb bombs. While the fuselages looked similar to those of the P-51H, they featured an extra section, some 4ft 9in long, which was inserted aft of the radiator housing and forward of the tailplane.

While the first production mark of the Twin Mustang showed great promise, it never got the chance to fully prove itself, as the initial order for 500 P-82B aircraft was cut down to just 20 following the dropping of the atomic bomb on Hiroshima and Nagasaki and the subsequent VJ Day. 18 of the production batch went into service with the USAF Air Defence Command, while the remaining two were finished as P-82C and -D night fighter variants and were evaluated as replacements for the Northrop P-61 Black Widow.

However, orders were forthcoming for the -C, -D and -E models, the latter being fitted with a pair of Allison engines, and these saw service with the newly established Strategic Air Command. Providing sterling service during the Korean War (along with standard P-51s), in fighter, photographic reconnaissance and radar-equipped night fighter modes, the Twin Mustang never really basked in the glory captured by its single-engined sister. Having said that, it was well liked by those who flew it and its role was really only made obsolete by the advent of suitable jet aircraft

Into The Post-War Years
The end of World War Two and the advent of jet-powered fighters brought a time of mixed fortunes for the Mustang. The RAF retired the type from active service relatively quickly, which was partly due to the wartime arrangement of 'Lend-Lease', whereby aircraft had to be returned to the USA, or purchased by the operating country.

In the USA the Mustang actually gained a new lease of life, when, after being withdrawn from front line fighting units, in favour of the up and coming more advanced jet fighters, it soon started to equip the US Air National Guard (ANG) squadrons. Before long it had become the

Above: This head-on view shows just how streamlined and 'clean' the P-51D Mustang airframe was. Note that this aircraft has the standard fit of six machine guns, and also carries the attachment points for long-range fuel tanks under the wings. (Key Collection)

Below: Wartime colour image of P-51D 44-13704 *Ferocious Frankie* of the 374th Fighter Squadron, 361st Fighter Group, dropping a couple of 500lb bombs during a mission out of its Little Walden base. Flown by 'ace' pilot Lt Col Wallace E Hopkins, who was credited with eight confirmed victories, the fighter was named after his wife! This identical paint scheme is currently worn by the Duxford-based Old Flying Machine Company's P-51D 44-73149 (G-BTCD), which forms part of the famed Breitling Fighters Team. (US National Archives)

most widely used type within the organisation. Mustangs soldiered on with the ANG until February 14, 1957, when P-51D 44-72948 was officially retired from service with the West Virginia ANG. This was the last active Mustang in the USAF inventory.

During the Korean War the Mustang gained a new lease of life, when as many aircraft as possible were gathered together for use by front-line units in the air operations over South Korea (see separate chapter)

Sale of surplus Mustangs to foreign air forces also took place in the immediate post-war years. 50 were supplied to China and 40 were operated by the Netherlands East Indies Air Force. The Royal Swedish Air Force was one of the biggest post-war Mustang operators. During World War Two several Mustangs had made

emergency landings in neutral Sweden and had been interned there for the duration.

At the end of the war, the Royal Swedish Air Force (RSAF) took two of these interned airframes on charge, gave them the designation J26, and flew them on evaluation trials. Following what turned out to be satisfactory tests, orders for 157 P-51Ds were placed in the USA. With deliveries of the fighters completed by 1948, the Mustangs only remained in service until 1952, when they were retired due to the RSAF taking on charge new jet fighters. The RSAF P-51s were subsequently purchased by air arms in Latin America and Israel. Other countries which operated the Mustang included: Australia (where the type was licence-built by the Commonwealth Aircraft Corporation), Bolivia, Canada, Costa Rica, Cuba, Dominican Republic, El

Above: Flown during World War Two by the 374th Fighter Squadron's Lt-Col Wallace Hopkins, P-51D 44-13704 *Ferocious Frankie* lives on today, as these markings are currently being worn by the Old Flying Machine Company's P-51D G-BTCD. The fighter flies as part of the famed Breitling Fighter Team. (Pete West)

Left: It wasn't just American bombers that Mustangs escorted! Here a P-51D of the Leiston-based 357th Fighter Group keeps an eye on a 'wounded' Royal Air Force Halifax. (Keith Hill Studios – www.KeithHillStudios.co.uk)

Below: The Mustangs could not have operated to the extent that they did without the support of the hard-working groundcrew. Here, Lt A Gundy of the 352nd Fighter Squadron, poses with his groundcrew alongside 'their' P-51D *Alabama Rammer Jammer.* (US National Archives)

Above: Groundcrews toiled night and day to make sure their 'charges' were ready for operations. During the *D-Day* campaign Staff Sergeant Gerald Bentley and a colleague carry out essential maintenance on the Merlin engine of this yellow-nosed P-51D.

Salvador, Guatemala, Haiti, Honduras, Indonesia, Israel, Italy, the Netherlands, New Zealand, Nicaragua, the Philippines, South Africa, Switzerland and Uruguay.

Of these the Dominican Republic was the last air force to fly the Mustang operationally, the type remaining in service for an incredible 36 years and only being retired as late as 1984. Over the years the P-51s worked hard and were often operated in anger against Bolivia's Cuban adversaries. Operational attrition accounted for a number of airframes and the final years of the type's military career in Dominica saw just over one squadron's-worth in regular use. In 1984 all of the aircraft were offered for sale on the civilian marketplace and were swiftly purchased by

American businessman Brian O'Farrell. These machines were then restored for civilian use and quickly sold on to private owners, joining the increasing numbers of airworthy Mustang warbirds in the USA.

In 1967 the US Department of Defence issued a contract to the Cavalier Aircraft Corporation, based at Sarasota in Florida, to re-work 15 F-51Ds, including one two-seat TF-51D trainer. Major overhauls were carried out on the airframes and engines, and the rejuvenated aircraft emerged as the Cavalier Mustang II. These variants featured extended tail 'feathers' for improved directional stability. The wing was also modified to carry a pair of fixed 110 US gallon tip tanks, plus 2,000 lbs (907.2kg) of ordnance. Cavalier also sold converted Mustangs to foreign air forces, where they were used in a variety of roles, including counter-insurgency. Sales to civilians were also forthcoming for this new addition to the P-51 range and a number were sold to private individuals who wanted a high-speed aircraft which could be used for business and pleasure. Fitted with modern avionics, leather seats and extra soundproofing, these aircraft were certainly status symbols, when compared with the rather ordinary and sedate Cessna or Piper business aircraft of the period!

The ultimate variant of the wartime fighter icon came in the shape of the turboprop-powered Cavalier Turbo

Left: Conditions during the Korean War were not always conducive to 'normal' operations. This USAF F-51 Mustang, 44-64004, taxies out through a somewhat 'damp' area of the airfield. (US National Archives)

Below: '13-K' was one of ten F-51Ds donated to the Republic of South Korea Air Force under Project Bout One. The aircraft arrived at Taegu, South Korea, on June 30, 1950, and needless to say was soon flying operational missions. (Pete West)

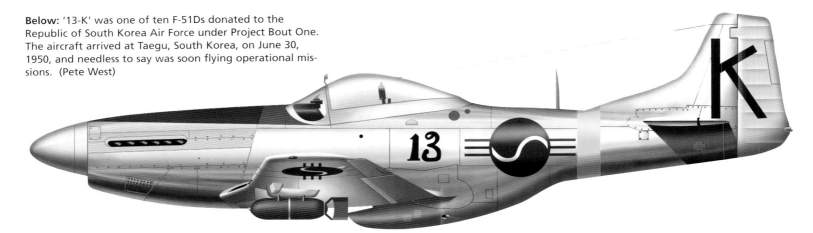

Mustang III. A 1,740shp (1,298kW) Rolls Royce Dart engine, along with its Dowty-Rotol propeller, taken from a British-designed Vickers Viscount airliner were mated to the P-51 airframe. The cockpit benefitted from a complete upgrade in terms of instrumentation and communications equipment and the fighter's wings were strengthened to be able to carry four 250lb (113.4kg) bombs. Production of two more Turbo Mustang IIIs was taken on by Piper Aircraft, resulting in the Piper PA-48 Enforcer. Unfortunately the first Enforcer crashed in July 1971, but the second airframe was evaluated by the USAF as a light attack and counter insurgency aircraft. After a number of trials, no production orders were forthcoming and the Enforcer programmme was cancelled.

This then was the last of the breed, a far cry from the Allison-powered aircraft which first flew in October 1940. The Mustang's development was complete and the fighter which had, in terms of its military service, acquitted itself well in World War Two and the Korean War, faded into the history books. A new chapter, as a civilian-operated aircraft, has continued to this day.

The Warbird Scene

It was fairly obvious that the Mustang would always hold a place in the hearts of the American people, aviation

Left: The Swedish Air Force was one of several foreign operators of the P-51. This particular airframe, 44-63864, saw much operational service with the USAAF's 78th Fighter Group at Duxford, UK, during World War Two, its regular pilot, Lt Hubert Davis, even being awarded two kills. Shipped to Sweden after World War Two had ended, it has moved around the globe a fair bit since then. In 1954 it went to Israel and saw service with the Israeli Defence Force. After 'demob' it was operated for a while by a private owner in Israel as 4X-AIM, it then went back to Sweden where it was flown in private hands as SE-BKG, although it wore its Swedish Air Force markings. In April 2002 it returned to the UK and is now operated by The Fighter Collection at Duxford, its former wartime base. (Key – Ken Delve)

Bottom: Final military operator of the Mustang was the Dominican Republic. P-51s served with the air arm of this country for an incredible 36 years and were finally retired in 1984. This poor quality, but historically interesting, view shows the F-51s wearing the distinctive two-tone green camouflage pattern adopted by the Fuerza Aerea Dominicana. (Key Collection)

Right: During the latter part of World War Two an unusual development of the P-51 was the P-82/F-82 Twin Mustang. Two Mustang fuselages were joined together using a new wing centre section and tailplane and the strange-looking aircraft was operated as an effective long-range fighter, although it was not built in large numbers. The P-82B pictured here, 44-65168 *Betty Joe*, gave a tangible demonstration of the Twin Mustang's long-range capabilities when, on February 28, 1947, it flew non-stop from Hickham Field, Hawaii, to La Guardia Airport, New York, a distance of 4,968 miles (7,995km). An extra fuel tank was installed behind the pilot's seat in each fuselage, as well as four wing-mounted drop tanks, giving the aircraft a total fuel capacity of 2,215 US gallons. No autopilot was fitted, so the two pilots had to share the 14 hours and 31 minutes of flying between them. An impressive task to say the least! (US National Archives)

enthusiasts and former wartime aviators. So much so that when P-51s started to become available as 'civilian' aircraft, it soon became apparent that those with enough money who wanted to re-live their wartime flying careers, or those who just wanted to sample what these powerful aircraft were like to fly, would acquire examples and keep them in airworthy condition.

This was the start of the 'warbird scene', which has now grown so large, worldwide, it has become a flourishing 'industry'. One of the first organisations to acquire a Mustang (indeed it was one of the founding aircraft types) was the Texas-based Confederate Air Force (CAF). A bunch of Texan pilots clubbed together and purchased a Curtiss P-40 Warhawk purely for recreational flying purposes. After a couple of years they felt the need for something more powerful and found that P-51D 44-73843 (N10601) was available for sale. After buying and flying the aircraft for a while, and thoroughly enjoying themselves in the process, legend has it that one night someone painted the name Confederate Air Force underneath the tail of the fighter and the CAF was born. This was back in 1957 and today the CAF (now re-named Commemorative Air Force) has grown into one of the largest operators of former World War Two fighters and bombers in the world.

While in the late 1950s and 1960s the purchase price of an aircraft like a Mustang was not too expensive, but as the years have passed the prices of World War Two aircraft have increased dramatically. Whole industries have now sprung up catering for those wealthy people who want an example of America's most famous World War Two fighter restored to flyable condition. Each year more and more Mustangs take to the skies again and one only has to look at the listings of surviving aircraft, elsewhere in this book, to judge for yourself the interest and enthusiasm for the famed North American product.

The P-51 Mustang has deservedly become a living legend and tales of its wartime exploits continue to enthrall those who listen to the surviving pilots of World War Two. At airshows and air events all over the world the classic shape and distinctive sound of the Mustang continues to bring enjoyment to those who are privileged to witness this icon of the skies performing in its natural element. Next to the Supermarine Spitfire it is the World War Two fighter aircraft that most private pilots would give almost anything to be able to get into its cockpit and take it for a flight. Now, over 60 years after its inception, the P-51 still reins supreme!

Right: Just a handful of Twin Mustangs survive today. This example, 44-65162 (N12102) was operated by the Midland, Texas, USA-based Commemorative Air Force for many years until it was traded in 2002 for an airworthy Lockheed P-38 Lightning. This view of the, then all-black painted, F-82 was taken at one of the CAF's air displays at Harlingen in the mid 1980s, before the organisation moved to Midland. Experiencing a crash landing at Harlingen in October 1987, many subsequent efforts were made to raise the funding required to put this distinctive aircraft back into the air, but to no avail. It never flew again during the rest of its time in CAF hands! (Key – Duncan Cubitt)

Left: In the mid to late 1960s the single-engined Mustang emerged again, this time modified by the Cavalier Aircraft Corporation, for use by foreign air forces, or private individuals who wanted a high-speed aircraft which could be used for business and pleasure. This example, NL51DH, was photographed at Oshkosh in 1995, and still retains its Cavalier modifications, such as the wingtip fuel tanks, taller fin and rudder, and tinted cockpit canopy. (Key – Ken Delve)

Centre: Last variant in the Mustang breed was the Piper PA-48 Enforcer. A turboprop-powered version of the F-51, the Enforcer was put forward as a ground attack and counter insurgency aircraft but was never put into production. It therefore quickly faded into obscurity. This example, N432PE, is pictured in storage at Davis-Monthan Air Force Base, Arizona, USA. (Key – Duncan Cubitt)

Bottom: As a preserved warbird the P-51 Mustang currently goes from strength to strength. More and more airframes take to the skies again each year, providing a living reminder of one of the world's greatest fighting aircraft of all time. One of the more recent rebuilds is this aircraft, 42-103645 (NL61429), a P-51C, which is operated by the Commemorative Air Force. It wears the markings of the USAAF's 302nd Fighter Squadron, 332nd Fighter Group, 15th Air Force, the only Negro-manned unit to fly with the air force during World War Two. Nicknamed the *Tuskegee Airmen,* all of the aircraft in the 302nd FS wore these distinctive red tail colours. After many years of detailed restoration work, this aircraft flew again (for the first time in 56 years) on May 10, 2001, and is a fine tribute to all who went to war in the North American P-51 Mustang. (Key – Steve Fletcher)

Right: The Fighter Collection's Duxford, Cambs-based P-51C '2106449' (G-PSIC) is painted in the markings carried by the P-51B flown by 1st Lt William Whisner, a pilot with the US 8th Air Force's 487th Fighter Squadron, 352nd Fighter Group. Coded HO-W, the aircraft also bears the legend *Princess Elizabeth* on the port engine cowling. (Key – Ken Delve)

Above: The main airframe used in this chapter is the Duxford, UK-based P-51D Mustang '463221' (G-BTCD). Originally operated in the UK by The Fighter Collection, in recent years it has appeared in the hands of the Old Flying Machine Company (OFMC). It is pictured here at La Ferte Alias, France, in 1999, being flown by OFMC's Nigel Lamb. (Key – Duncan Cubitt)

Right: The ideal time to generate a detailed 'walk around' series of illustrations is during an aircraft's major maintenance schedule. We caught the OFMC's Mustang during its winter overhaul period and this view serves to illustrate just how accessible the P-51 was to those who had to look after its inner workings. (Key – Duncan Cubitt)

Left: The P-51s beautifully contoured underbelly radiator housing takes on a whole new look when it is dismantled. The main coolant radiator has been removed in this shot, leaving just the retaining straps in view. The myriad of tubing and piping surrounding the oil cooler (positioned in the housing below the aircraft's code letters) can clearly be seen. (Key – Duncan Cubitt)

Left: Minus its rudder and fuselage-to-tail fairing one can see the construction method for the tail area. The small hatch above the three-digit number reveals the cable arrangement for the rudder trim tab, while ballast weights are fitted to the rudder stern post. These weights are crucial to the fighter's centre of gravity. (Key – Duncan Cubitt)

Below: Viewed from the front, the smaller oil cooler radiator can be discerned, while the larger air intake area leading to the main coolant radiator is readily apparent. As with any World War Two aircraft, which was fitted with a liquid cooled engine, the problem of where to put the radiator where it would be least vulnerable was never really solved. Housing the Mustang's 'rad' in a streamlined under-fuselage housing was good for the aerodynamic aspect, but it was susceptible to damage from ground fire when the aircraft was operated on low-level missions. (Key – Duncan Cubitt)

Above: On the early marks of Mustang, the aircraft featured a 'high-back' fuselage, with a framed cockpit canopy, as shown on this example, The Fighter Collection's P-51C '2106449' (G-PSIC) *Princess Elizabeth.* Pilots who flew this variant during World War Two found the rearward view from the cockpit rather restricted. *India Charlie* made its UK display debut at Duxford's Flying Legends Airshow in July 1997. (Key – Robert J Rudhall)

Right: Just forward of where the rear fuselage joins the main section, a hole goes straight through the airframe. This is so the aircraft can be jacked up off the ground, as can be seen in this view. During this Mustang's maintenance schedule the tailwheel and its strut had been removed, leaving just the open tailwheel doors. (Key – Duncan Cubitt)

Above: With the teardrop hood removed the canopy attachment rails can be seen, along with the modern-day GPS (Global Positioning System) antenna at the rear of the cockpit. (Key – Duncan Cubitt)

Left: The one-piece teardrop canopy of the P-51D was a revelation for the pilots who flew this machine in combat. Out went the heavy framed canopy of the earlier –B and –C models and in came the superb all-round view from the 'blown' Perspex hood. This Mustang, 44-73264 (N5428V) is operated by Omaha. Nebraska, USA-based Regis Urschler, a 'Colonel' in the Texas-based Commemorative Air Force. Note the rear view mirror attached to the starboard windscreen strut. (Key – Duncan Cubitt)

Below: Minus its main wheel assembly, the one-strut undercarriage can be viewed in this semi-dismantled condition. The inward-retracting undercarriage legs are operated by a system of actuating links and pulleys. The landing light, attached to the rear of the bay automatically lowers when the main gear is in the down position. (Key – Duncan Cubitt)

Right: The main undercarriage wheel well contains a mass of piping, all of which can have serious implications to the fighter's airworthiness if damaged. In the top/centre position in the bay is the undercarriage up-lock hook, while the jack for retracting the main doors can be seen on the left bulkhead. These two main doors, which enclose the wheels when in flight, are operated in sequence by a series of cables. They droop down when the aircraft is at rest, due to there being no pressure in the hydraulic system. (Key – Duncan Cubitt)

Below: The flap actuating mechanism is pictured here in a disconnected state, hence the flap hanging down almost vertically. This view also shows the coolant piping making its way underneath the cockpit from the engine to the radiator housing. (Key – Duncan Cubitt)

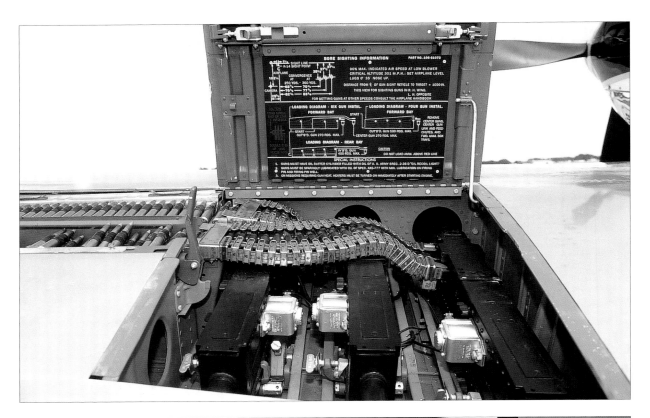

Left: The P-51s gun access bays are located on the upper surface of the wing. Several of today's airworthy Mustangs have these areas fully fitted out in stock military configuration. This aircraft, 44-72438 (N7551T), is Bob Jepson's Kissimmee, Florida, USA-based *Lady Alice*. In 1997, while operated by Selby Burch, it won the Grand Champion Warbird award at Lakeland's Sun 'n Fun fly-in event. Looking at the detail within the gun bays alone, it is not surprising the Mustang was a winner! (Key – Duncan Cubitt)

Below: Another view of *Lady Alice's* gun bay, showing that even the bore sighting information and loading diagram plaque has been faithfully replicated on the wing access panel. (Key – Duncan Cubitt)

Top right: Heart of the Mustang, a Rolls Royce Merlin! The engine fitted to the OFMC's P-51D is a Merlin 724, and is believed to have originally been fitted to an Avro York transport aircraft. The trunking arrangement at the bottom of the engine is the carburettor air intake ducting, the grey tank mounted on the engine bulkhead at the rear of the Merlin contains engine oil and the various engine-driven pumps can be clearly seen on the side of the Merlin. This view also highlights just how closely-cowled the Mustang's Merlin was, affording the fighter its smooth streamlined frontal area. (Key – Duncan Cubitt)

Right: Immaculately turned out in its moveable trolley, this example of the mighty Merlin is kept as a showpiece at the Stallion 51 Corp's facility at Kissimmee, Florida, USA. Whichever way you look at it, the Merlin is a large chunk of metal! (Key – Duncan Cubitt)

Left: The propeller unit, without which no Mustang would get very far. This shot, minus the front section of the spinner, reveals the blade attachment details, plus the dome, forward of the actual propeller blades, which contains the Constant Speed Unit. This motor, powered by oil pressure, changes the angle of the propeller blades for any given engine power setting. This ensures that the propeller blades are always set at the most efficient angle. (Key – Duncan Cubitt)

Below: The 'office'. With the pilot's seat removed, a far better view can be had of the Mustang's cockpit. Roomy by wartime standards (it had to be as some missions could take as long as eight hours!), the P-51 cockpit is still fairly typical of a World War Two fighter's interior. Instruments were laid out on the panel in a reasonably organised manner. The throttle, rudder, aileron and elevator trim tab wheels can be seen on the port fuselage wall and lower panel, while the modern radio is positioned on the starboard side of the cockpit, as is the canopy winding handle. On original wartime Mustangs the radio was situated behind the pilots seat, the transmitters and receivers of those days being much larger than the compact units of today. Key – Duncan Cubitt)

Right: A dramatic difference to the previous illustration, this shot shows the two-place cockpit arrangement fitted to Stallion 51's TF-51 Mustang 44-848745 (NL851D) *Crazy Horse*. A training variant of the Mustang fighter, the TF-51 has two complete instrument suites, along with throttle, undercarriage and flap controls situated in both pilot positions, and is the ideal mount for budding Mustang pilots to convert to the famed fighter. (Key – Duncan Cubitt)

MUSTANG VARIANTS AND DEVELOPMENT

Compared to many aircraft of its era the Mustang evolved through a relatively small number of different variants/marks. The quantum leap in its effectiveness came when the airframe was adapted to take the tried and trusted Rolls Royce Merlin engine. From then on the P-51 never looked back and quite literally led the field in wartime fighter performance and capabilities.

Over 14,000 Mustangs were produced, the type accounting for 4,950 air kills, 4,131 ground kills, plus 230 V.1 flying bomb kills.

Below: General three-view drawing of the North American P-51A, or Mustang I, as the RAF named it. (Key Collection)

North American NA-73X/Mustang I/XP- 51/Mustang IA/P-51 Apache	
Powerplant	1,150hp Allison V-1710-39 liquid cooled V-12 engine driving a three-blade constant speed Curtiss propeller.
Dimensions	
Wingspan:	37ft 0.3in,
Length:	32ft 3in
Height:	11ft 9in
Wing area:	235.75sq ft.
Weights	
Empty:	6,270lb
Loaded:	7,908lb
Fuel:	180 Gall (in wing tanks)
	Mustang 1A/P-51
Empty:	6,550lb
Loaded:	7,580lb
Armament	Eight machine guns. Two 0.50-in guns below engine, one 0.50-in and two 0.30-in guns in each wing.
	Mustang IA/P-51
	Four 200-mm cannons, two in each wing
Performance	
Cruising speed:	325mph
Maximum speed:	375mph
Landing speed:	83mph
Range:	640-1,022 miles
	Mustang IA/P-51
Crusing speed (fully loaded):	307mph
Landing speed:	90mph
Rate of Climb:	1,600ft/min
Service ceiling:	31,350ft
Range:	350-1,175 miles

Above: After the unfortunate crash of the prototype, flight-testing continued on the first example (AG345) from the Royal Air Force's first order of 320 Mustang I airframes. (Key Collection)

Below: For its day the NA-73X was a sleek machine. Note the extremely low frontal area, due to the streamlined engine cowlings, which would alter slightly once the aircraft entered service, as would the under-fuselage radiator housing. (Key Collection)

P-51B/C Mustang (RAF Mustang III)	
Powerplant	1,380hp Packard/Rolls Royce V-1650-3 Merlin V-12 liquid cooled engine driving a four-blade Hamilton Standard Hydromatic propeller
Dimensions	As per Mustang I/XP-51/Mustang Ia/P-51 Apache
Weights	
Empty:	6,933lb
Loaded:	9,600lb
	Fuel: 180 gallons in wing tanks and 85 gallons in auxiliary fuselage tank, plus two 150-gall drop tanks, or two 300-gall ferry tanks
Armament	As per P-51A
Performance	
Cruising speed:	362mph
Maximum speed:	440mph
Landing speed:	100mph
Rate of Climb:	2,500ft/min
Service ceiling:	41,800ft
Range:	1,450-2,650 miles

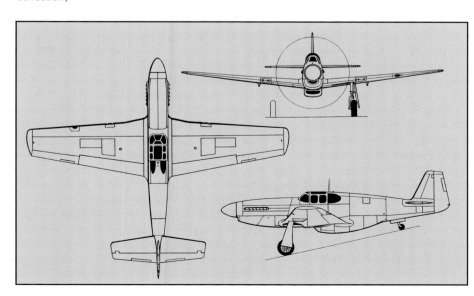

Above: This view of P-51B 43-12408 illustrates the differences between the Allison-engined aircraft and the Merlin-powered Mustang. The air intake has been deleted from the top engine cowling, the Merlin's exhausts stacks are located higher on the side cowlings than the Allison's and the under-fuselage radiator housing is deeper. (Key Collection)

Above right: The RAF's 2 Squadron operated Mustangs from 1942 onwards and the aircraft were initially flown in the Army Co-operation/Tactical Reconnaissance roles. AG633 displays its sideways-looking camera port, just behind the cockpit (above the letter X). (Key Collection)

Below: P-51B Mustang three-view drawing. The almost flat cockpit canopy, with its multiple glazing panels, precluded the pilots from having a good view, especially to the rear of the aircraft. This would be changed with the next major variant, the P-51D. (Key Collection)

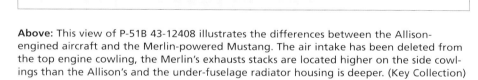

P-51A Mustang/RAF Mustang III/A-36 Invader	
Powerplant	1,200hp Allison V-1710-81, (A-36) 1,325hp V-1710-87
Dimensions	As per Mustang I/XP-51/Mustang Ia/P-51 Apache
Weights	
Empty:	6,700lb
Loaded:	9,600lb
A-36	
Empty:	6,736lbs
Loaded:	8,370lbs
	Maximum All Up Weight: 10,700lb (with two 75 gall drop tanks or two 150-gall long-range ferry tanks)
Armament	Four 0.50-in machine guns, two in each wing.
A-36	
	Six 0.50-in guns, two in each wing. One 250lb, 300lb or 500lb bomb under each wing
Performance	
Cruising speed:	315mph
Maximum speed:	390mph
Landing speed:	86mph
Rate of Climb:	1,650ft/min
Service ceiling:	31,350ft
Range:	750-1,290 miles (combat), 2,350 miles (ferry)
A-36	
Cruising speed:	312mph
Maximum speed:	360mph
Rate of Climb:	2,700ft/min
Service ceiling:	27,300ft
Range:	775-1,290miles

XP-51F/XP-51G/XP-51J Mustang (RAF Mustang V [XP-51F], VI [XP-51G])

Powerplant

(XP-51F): 1,380hp Packard/Rolls Royce V-1650-3 liquid cooled Merlin engine driving a three-blade Aeroproducts propeller, (XP-51G): 1,650hp Rolls Royce RM.14SM driving a three-blade Aeroproducts or five-blade Rotol propeller, (XP-51J): 1,720hp V-1710-119 driving four-blade Aeroproducts propeller

Dimensions

Wingspan: 37ft 0.3in

Length: 32ft 3in (XP-51J) 33ft

Weights

(XP-51F)

Empty: 5,635lb

Loaded: 6,296lb

Fuel: 180 gallons in wing tanks

(XP-51G)

Empty: 5,750lb

Loaded: 7,860lb

(XP-51J)

Empty: 5,750lb

Loaded: 7,400lb

Armament

(XP-51F and J): Four 0.50-in machine guns, two in each wing. (XP-51G): Six 0.50-in machine guns, three in each wing

Performance

(XP-51F)

Cruising speed: 380mph

Maximum speed: 466mph at 29,000ft, 491mph at 21,500ft

Landing speed: 85mph

Rate of Climb: 4,000ft/min

Service ceiling: 42,100ft

Range: 1,112 miles

(XP-51G)

Maximum speed: 498mph

Rate of Climb: 5,800ft/min

Service ceiling: 45,000ft

Range: 510 miles

(XP-51J)

Maximum speed: 491mph

P-51D/K/M Mustang (RAF Mustang IV)/TF-51D

Powerplant P-51D/K 1,490hp Packard/Rolls Royce V-1650-7 liquid cooled Merlin engine (P-51M) V-1650-9A, driving a four-blade Aeroproducts propeller

Dimensions As per Mustang I/XP-51/Mustang Ia/P-51 Apache

Weights

Empty: 7,125lb

Loaded: 10,100lb

Fuel: as per P-51B/C, except two 75-gallon drop tanks, or two 108-gallon paper tanks

Armament Six 0.50-in machine guns, three in each wing. One 100 to 1,000lb bomb or five 5-in HVAR rockets under each wing

Performance

Cruising speed: 363mph

Maximum speed: 437mph

Landing speed: 100mph

Rate of Climb: 3,450ft/min

Service ceiling: 41,900ft

Range: 950-2,300 miles

Below: In order to alleviate the rearward visibility problem some Mustang IIIs were fitted with the 'blown' Malcolm canopy, similar to that fitted to the British Spitfire fighter. This aircraft, FX893, has been fitted with rocket rails for trials work. When this experimental task was completed the aircraft was sent to the Middle East. (Key Collection)

Bottom: Long-range drop tanks were fitted underneath the wing of RAF Mustang III FX898. This well-worn aircraft still sports the framed P-51B-style cockpit canopy. (Key Collection)

Right: An evocative view of a P-51D Mustang, devoid of any national markings. The –D model was really the best of the P-51 bunch. Rolls Royce/Packard Merlin engine, six machine guns, extra fuel tanks, the fighter had it all! With its long range and effective firepower these fighters ranged far and wide over Europe in the closing stages of World War Two, escorting bombers, strafing ground targets and generally causing havoc to the Axis forces. Note that this aircraft has been fitted with the fin fillet, which was to characterise the P-51s tail area for the rest of its military career. (Key collection)

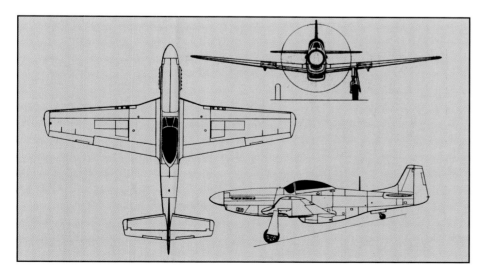

Above centre:, the quintessential Mustang. 44-13341 was part of a batch of 800 P-51D-5NA's built by North American Aviation. This airframe must have been one of the early –D models, as it has not been fitted with the extra fin fillet, which was added to give better directional stability. (Key Collection)

Above: The P-51D. It is this model which makes up the bulk of today's preserved Mustangs, although there are a handful of Allison-engined high-back variants which have been restored in recent years. (Key Collection)

P-51H/F-51H Mustang	
Powerplant	1,380hp Packard/Rolls Royce Merlin V-1650-9 liquid cooled engine, driving a four-blade Aeroproducts propeller
Dimensions	
Wingspan:	37ft 0.3in
Length:	33ft 4in
Weights	
Empty:	6,481lb
Loaded:	9,465lb
Fuel:	117 gallons in wing tanks, 50 gallons in a uxiliary fuselage tank, two 75, 110 or 165 gallon drop tanks
Armament:	Six 0.50-in machine guns, three in each wing
Performance	
Cruising speed:	380mph
Maximum speed:	487mph
Landing speed:	96mph
Rate of Climb:	2,400ft/min
Service ceiling:	41,600ft
Range:	945 miles

RF-51D (formerly an F-6D) of the 45th TRS, 67th TRW, which operated out of Taegu (K-2) in mid-1951. Oblique and vertical cameras were mounted in the aircraft's rear fuselage and it went on to carry out some 30 operational missions, as depicted by the small camera symbols below the cockpit. (Pete West)

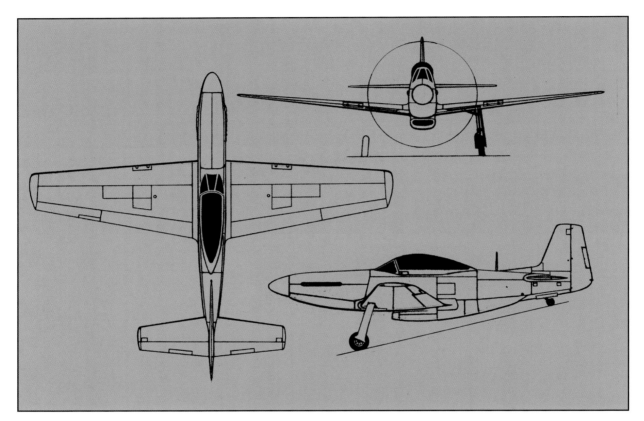

Left: The XP-51J was quite a different beast from the earlier marks. The kink in the leading edge of the wing, near the fuselage, has gone and the aircraft has a different undercarriage arrangement, with modified main gear and a tailwheel positioned more towards the rear of the aircraft. These alterations, and a longer cockpit canopy, made for a radical departure to the previous Mustang design 'signatures'. (Key Collection)

Below: P-51Ds as far as the eye can see! Mustangs of the USAF's 7th Fighter Squadron, 49th Fighter Group, line-up on parade in 1946. The aircraft nearest the camera, *Charlote Jeanne,* is the mount of Major James A Watkins. (Warren Thompson Collection)

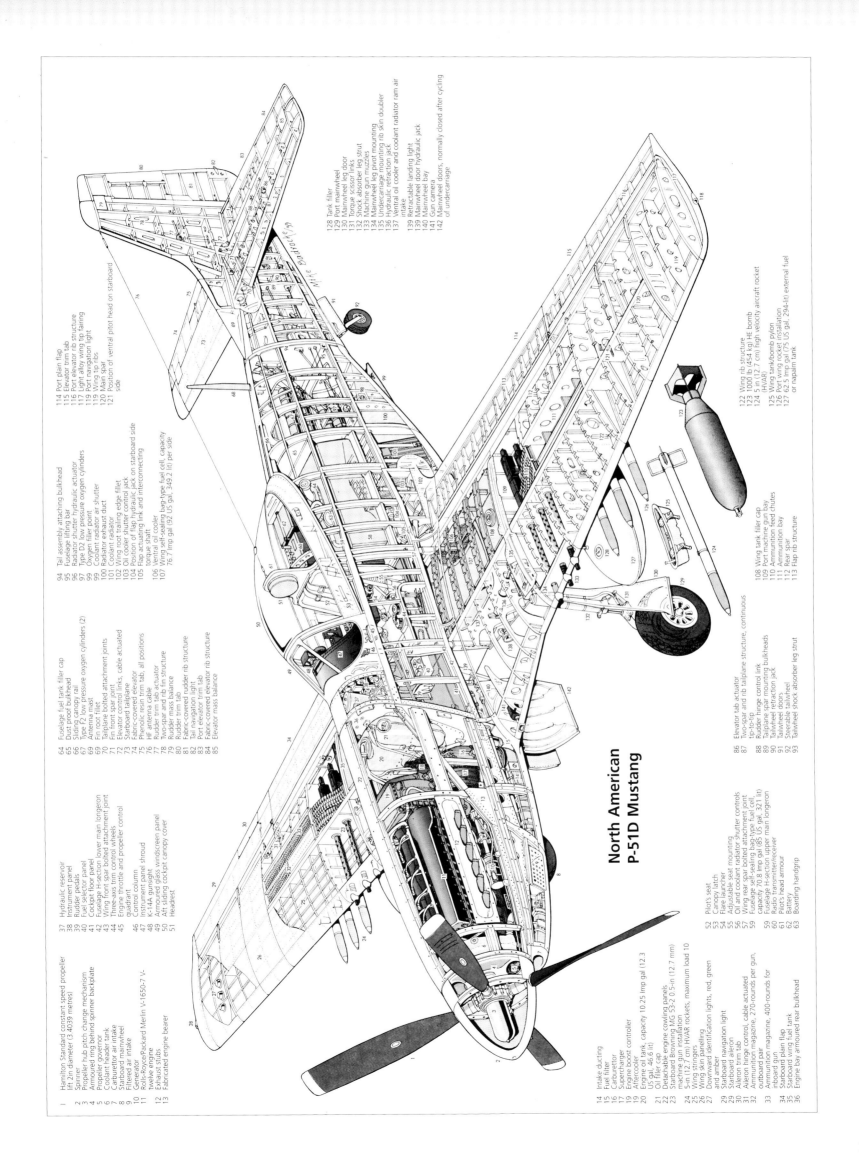

**North American
P-51D Mustang**

1 Hamilton Standard constant speed propeller lift 2in diameter (3.4039 metres)
2 Spinner
3 Propeller hub pitch change mechanism
4 Armoured ring behind spinner backplate
5 Propeller governor
6 Carburettor air intake
7 Coolant header tank
8 Starboard mainwheel
9 Filtered air intake
10 Generator
11 Rolls-Royce/Packard Merlin V-1650-7 V-twelve engine
12 Exhaust stubs
13 Fabricated engine bearer

14 Intake ducting
15 Fuel filter
16 Carburettor
17 Supercharger
18 Engine boost controller
19 Aftercooler
20 Engine oil tank, capacity 10.25 Imp gal (12.3 US gal, 46.6 lit)
21 Oil filler cap
22 Detachable engine cowling panels
23 Starboard Browning MG 53-2 0.5-in (12.7 mm) machine gun installation
24 5-in (12.7 cm) HVAR rockets, maximum load 10
25 Wing stringers
26 Wing skin panelling
27 Downward identification lights, red, green and amber
29 Starboard navigation light
30 Starboard aileron
31 Aileron hinge control, cable actuated
32 Ammunition magazine, 270-rounds per gun, outboard pair
33 Ammunition magazine, 400-rounds for inboard gun
34 Starboard plain flap
35 Starboard wing fuel tank
36 Engine bay armoured rear bulkhead

37 Hydraulic reservoir
38 Instrument panel
39 Rudder pedals
41 Fuel selector panel
42 Cockpit floor panel
43 Fuselage H-section lower main longeron
44 Wing front spar bolted attachment joint
45 Engine throttle and propeller control quadrant
46 Control column
47 Instrument panel shroud
48 K-14A gunsight
49 Armoured glass windscreen panel
50 Aft sliding cockpit canopy cover
51 Headrest

52 Pilot's seat
53 Canopy latch
54 Flare launcher
55 Adjustable seat mounting
56 Oil and coolant radiator shutter controls
57 Wing rear spar bolted attachment joint
59 Fuselage self-sealing bag-type fuel cell, capacity 70.8 Imp gal (85 US gal, 321 lit)
59 Fuselage H-section upper main longeron
60 Radio transmitter/receiver
61 Pilot's head armour
62 Battery
63 Boarding handgrip

64 Fuselage fuel tank filler cap
65 Dust proof bulkhead
66 Sliding canopy rail
67 Type F2 low pressure oxygen cylinders
69 Fin root fillet
69 Antenna mast
70 Tailplane bolted attachment joints
71 Fin front spar joint
72 Elevator control links, cable actuated
73 Starboard tailplane
74 Fabric-covered elevator
75 Phenolic resin trim tab, all positions
76 Rudder trim tab actuator
78 Two-spar and rib fin structure
79 Rudder trim tab
80 Rudder trim tab
81 Fabric-covered rudder rib structure
82 Tail navigation light
83 Port elevator trim tab
84 Fabric-covered elevator rib structure
85 Elevator mass balance

86 Elevator tab actuator
87 Two-spar and rib tailplane structure, continuous tip-to-tip
88 Rudder hinge control link
89 Tailplane spar mounting bulkheads
90 Tailwheel retraction jack
91 Tailwheel doors
92 Steerable tailwheel
93 Tailwheel shock absorber leg strut

94 Tail assembly attaching bulkhead
95 Fuselage lifting bar
96 Radiator shutter hydraulic actuator
97 Type D2 low pressure oxygen cylinders
99 Oxygen filler point
99 Coolant radiator air shutter
100 Radiator exhaust duct
101 Coolant radiator
102 Wing root trailing edge fillet
103 Oil cooler shutter control jack
104 Position of flap hydraulic jack on starboard side
105 Flap actuating link and interconnecting torque shaft
106 Ventral oil cooler
107 Wing self-sealing bag-type fuel cell, capacity 76.7 Imp gal (92 US gal, 349.2 lit) per side

108 Wing tank filler cap
109 Port machine gun bay
110 Ammunition feed chutes
111 Ammunition bay
112 Rear spar
113 Flap rib structure

114 Port plain flap
115 Elevator trim tab
116 Port elevator rib structure
117 Light alloy wing tip fairing
119 Port navigation light
119 Wing tip ribs
120 Main spar
121 Position of ventral pitot head on starboard side

122 Wing rib structure
123 1000 lb (454 kg) HE bomb
124 5-in (12.7 cm) high velocity aircraft rocket (HVAR)
125 Wing tankbomb pylon
126 Port wing rocket installation
127 62.5 Imp gal (75 US gal, 294-lit) external fuel or napalm tank

128 Tank filler
130 Port mainwheel
131 Mainwheel leg door
132 Torque scissor links
133 Shock absorber leg strut
133 Machine gun muzzles
134 Mainwheel leg pivot mounting
135 Undercarriage mounting rib skin doubler
137 Ventral oil cooler and coolant radiator ram air intake
139 Retractable landing light
139 Mainwheel door hydraulic jack
140 Mainwheel bay
141 Gun camera
142 Mainwheel doors, normally closed after cycling of undercarriage

Opposite page, top: Tom Blair's Potomac, Maryland-based Mustang '44-14812' (NL51DT) *Slender, Tender & Tall* heads up this overview of P-51 nose-art. When this photograph was taken the aircraft was in the ownership of Dick Thurman, who operated it in the markings carried by the P-51s of the USAAF's 352nd Fighter Group. The 352nd flew out of Bodney in the UK, plus Asche and Chievres in Belgium, between September 1943 and May 1945. (Key – Duncan Cubitt)

Opposite page, bottom: The late Paul Morgan's UK-based P-51D, 44-72773 (G-SUSY) *Susy* heads a line-up of the breed at the 1999 Flying Legends Airshow. Held each year at the Imperial War Museum's Duxford Airfield,

Cambs, this display always attracts a healthy number of Mustangs and the sight of up to eight examples indulging in a tailchase display can often be seen at the event. *Susy* sports the red nose of the USAAF 8th Air Force's 334th Fighter Group. (Key – Robert J Rudhall)

Above: Framed here by a vintage American Jeep, UK-based Rob Davies flies his Australian-built CAC-18 Mustang 22 A68-192 (G-HAEC) in the colours of the Duxford, UK-based 78th Fighter Group. The markings *Big Beautiful Doll* relate to the personal aircraft of Colonel John D Landers, the Group's Commanding Officer. (Key – Robert J Rudhall)

Above: This colour scheme and the nose logo *My Dallas Darlin* was specially applied to The Fighter Collection's P-51D 44-73149 (N51RR) for use in the 1987 film *Empire of the Sun.* The impressive, if short, aerial sequences in the film were shot on location near Jerez and Tablada in Spain. (Key – Duncan Cubitt)

Left: This close-up view of *Little One* shows to advantage the close cowling of the Mustang, and the shrouds around the engine exhaust. Not all Mustangs are fitted with these shrouds. This view also shows the exhaust 'bungs' often used by warbird owners to prevent moisture entering the engine while the aircraft is dormant. Sometimes purpose-built 'bungs' are used, while other occasions will see vending machine-style plastic cups being used for the same purpose! (Key – Robert J Rudhall)

Right: For many years this F-51 Mustang, 67-22581 (C-GMUS), was flown by Canadian-based Ross Grady and was a familiar sight at air events all over Canada and the USA. Named *What's Up Doc* after the famous Warner Bros cartoon character Bugs Bunny, the aircraft is pictured here taxying out at the Confederate (now Commemorative) Air Force's Southern Minnesota Wing's airshow, Holman Field, Minneapolis, in August 1995. Now registered as N151MC, the fighter is operated by the Gardner Capital Management Corp of New York. (Key – Duncan Cubitt)

Below: Bedecked in leather flying helmet and goggles, the carrot-chomping rabbit Bugs Bunny forms the centre-piece of the military-looking badge underneath the cockpit of *What's Up Doc*. (Key – Duncan Cubitt)

43

Left: Complete with 'whitewall' tyres, the Scandinavian Historic Flight's P-51D 44-73877 (N167F) flies as '414450' *Old Crow,* the wartime mount of famed ace Clarence Bud Anderson, who flew with the UK-based 357th Fighter Group, USAAF 8th Air Force. Flying for many years in a silver-style 357th scheme the Mustang adopted its more authentic olive drab colours in early 2001. (Key – Duncan Cubitt)

Below: *Montana Miss* features a scantily-clad cowgirl, brandishing a revolver, aptly reclining on snow-capped Montana mountains (which must be most uncomfortable!). This feast for the eyes adorns the nose of Edward Wachs' Lake Bluff, Illinois-based P-51K/F-6K Mustang 44-12840 (N51EW). (Key – Duncan Cubitt)

Above: The only razorback Mustang in this nose-art portfolio, The Fighter Collection's Duxford, UK-based P-51C 43-25147 (G-PSIC) wears markings which represent the aircraft flown by William Whisner while serving with the 487th Fighter Group. Completing two operational tours in the European Theatre of Operations, Whisner flew over 130 missions with the USAAF's 352nd FG. The legend *Princess Elizabeth* graces the nose of the Mustang and it is reported that Her Majesty The Queen saw Whisner's original aircraft during World War Two. This was, of course, a period when she was still Princess Elizabeth! (Key – Robert J Rudhall)

Right: One of a host of Mustangs, which regularly attend the EAA Fly-in at Oshkosh, Wisconsin, *Six-Shooter,* P-51D 67-22580 (N2580), is operated by Ramona, California-based Chuck Hall. A two-seat Cavalier conversion, the aircraft bears a rendition of the shotgun-smokin' Warner Bros cartoon character Yosemite Sam. (Key – Duncan Cubitt)

MUSTANG UNITS OF WORLD WAR TWO

United States Army Airforce

4th FG
Squadrons	334th, 335th and 336th FS
Air Force	8th AF
Aircraft	Spitfire Mk.V, P-47C/D, P-51B/D/K
Operational	Oct 1942 to May 1945
Bases	Debden, UK

20th FG
Squadrons	55th, 77th and 79th FS
Air Force	8th AF
Aircraft	P-38H/J, P-51C/D/K
Operational	Oct 1943 to May 1945
Bases	Kingscliffe, UK

31st FG
Squadrons	307th, 308th and 309th FS
Air Force	8th AF, 12th AF, 15th AF
Aircraft	Spitfire Mk.V, Mk.VIII, Mk.IX, P-51B/D
Operational	Aug 1942 to May 1945
Bases	Atcham, High Ercall, Westhampnett, Merston, UK; La Senia, Le Sers, Sbeitla, Tafaroui, Tebassa, Algeria; Gozo Island, Malta; Kalaa Djerda, Korba North, Thelepte, Youks-les-Bains, Tunisia; Aggrigento, Milazzo, Palerom, Ponte Olivo, Termini, Sicily; Castel Volturno, Mondolfo, Monte Corvino, Naples, Nettuno, Pomigliano, San Servo, Triolo, Italy

52nd FG
Squadrons	2nd, 4th and 5th FS
Air Force	8th AF, 12th AF, 15th AF
Aircraft	Spitfire Mk.V, P-51
Operational	Aug 1942 to May 1945
Bases	Eglington, Goxhill, UK; Tafaroui, La Senia, Bone, Orleansville, Biskra, Maison Blanche, Kalaa Djerda, Youks-les-Bains, Algeria; Thelepte, Telergma, Le Kouif, Tunis, Tunisia; Bocca di Falco, Sicily; Borgo, Calvi, Ghisonaccia, Corsica, Madna, Piagiolino, Italy

55th FG
Squadrons	38th, 338th and 343rd FS
Air Force	8th AF
Aircraft	P-38H/J, P-51D/K
Operational	Oct 1943 to May 1945
Bases	Nuthampstead, Wormingford, UK

78th FG
Squadrons	82nd, 83rd and 84th FS
Air Force	8th AF
Aircraft	P-38G, P-47C/D, P-51D/K
Operational	Apr 1943 to May 1945
Bases	Goxhill, Duxford, UK

Above: The pilot and crew of *"Davy Don Chariot"* stand alongside the drop tank-equipped P-51D of the 343rd Fighter Squadron, 55th Fighter Group, prior to the next mission. (US National Archives)

Below: Merlin-engined P-51B, 42-106886 *Swede,* saw service with the Fowlmere-based 339th Fighter Group. This artwork shows the aircraft as it would have appeared in October 1944. (Pete West)

Top Mustangs of the 350th Fighter Squadron sported distinctive black and yellow chequerboard nose markings. Pilot, Lt M Granger, poses for a 'snap' with his groundcrew members in front of *Lady Grace 3rd.* (US National Archives)

Above: Airborne from its Steeple Morden base, P-51D 44-13305 wears the WR codes of the 354th Fighter Squadron, 355th Fighter Group. Note the twin rear view mirrors mounted on top of the cockpit windscreen. (Key Collection)

Right: Capt W Price's *Janie* was one of the Mustangs operated by the 350FS, 353rd Fighter Group when based at Raydon, Suffolk. This particular colour scheme now adorns Maurice Hammond's beautifully restored P-51D '414419' (G-MSTG), which makes regular airshow appearances in the UK. (US National Archives)

Below: Lt J J Hagen flew *Dayton Demon* with the 353 Fighter Squadron, 354th Fighter Group during World War Two. Pictured during a visit to Croydon in the summer of 1945, Lt Hagen taxies 'his' P-51D out for take off. (L Hayes via Andrew Thomas)

86th FG	
Squadrons	311th, 525th, 526th and 527th FS
Air Force	12th AF
Aircraft	A-36, P-40, P-47D
Operational	July 1943 to May 1945
Bases	La Senia, Algeria; French Morocco; Tafaraoui, Algeria; Korba, Tunisia; Gela, Barcelona, Sicily; Sele, Serretella, Pomigliano, Marcianise, Ciampino, Orbetello, Italy; Corsica; Grosseto, Pisa, Italy; Tantonville, France; Braunschardt, Germany

325th FG	
Squadrons	317th, 318th and 319th FS
Air Force	12th AF, 15th AF
Aircraft	P-40F/L, P-47D, P-51D
Operational	Apr 1943 to May 1945
Bases	Tafaraoui, Montesquieu, Algeria; Souk el Khemis, Mateur, Soliman, Tunisia; Foggia, Celone, Lesina, Rimini, Mondolfo, Italy

332nd FG	
Squadrons	99th, 100th, 301st and 302nd FS
Air Force	12th AF, 15th AF
Aircraft	P-39, P-47D/P-51B/C
Operational	Apr 1944 to July 1944
Bases	Montecorvino, Capodichino, Ramitelli, Cattolica, Italy

339th FG	
Squadrons	503rd, 504th and 505th FS
Air Force	8th AF
Aircraft	P-51B/C/D/K
Operational	Apr 1944 to May 1945
Bases	Fowlmere, UK

352nd FG	
Squadrons	328th, 486th and 487th FS
Air Force	8th AF
Aircraft	P-47D, P-51B/C/D/K
Operational	Sept 1943 to May 1945
Bases	Bodney, UK; Asche, Chievres, Belgium

353rd FG	
Squadrons	350th, 351st and 352nd FS
Air Force	8th AF
Aircraft	P-47D, P-51D/K
Operational	Aug 1943 to May 1945
Bases	Goxhill, Metfield, Raydon, UK

354th FG

Squadrons	353rd, 355th and 356th FS
Air Force	9th AF
Aircraft	P-51, P-47D
Operational	Nov 1944 to Feb 1945
Bases	Greenham Common, Boxted, Lashenden, UK; Criqueville, Gael, France; Ober Olm, Herzogenaurach, Germany

355th FG

Squadrons	354th, 357th and 358th FS
Air Force	8th AF
Aircraft	P-47D, P-51B/D/K
Operational	Sept 1943 to May 1945
Bases	Steeple Morden, UK

356th FG

Squadrons	359th, 360th and 361st FS
Air Force	8th AF
Aircraft	P-47D, P-51D/K
Operational	Oct 1943 to May 1945
Bases	Goxhill, Martlesham Heath, UK

357th FG

Squadrons	362nd, 363rd and 364th FS
Air Force	8th AF, 9th AF
Aircraft	P-51B/C/K
Operational	Feb 1944 to May 1945
Bases	Raydon, Leiston, UK

359th FG

Squadrons	368th, 369th and 370th FS
Air Force	8th AF
Aircraft	P-47D, P-51B/C/D/K
Operational	Dec 1943 to May 1945
Bases	East Wretham, UK

361st FG

Squadrons	374th, 375th and 376th FS
Air Force	8th AF
Aircraft	P-47D, P-51B/C/D/K
Operational	Jan 1944 to May 1945
Bases	Bottisham, Little Walden, UK; St Dizier, France; Chievres, Belgium

Top: A couple of steel-helmeted ground-crew members watch a flight of four P-51Ds peel off before landing. Mustang 413309 *Fools Paradise IV* was at the time being operated by the 380th Fighter Squadron, 363rd Fighter Group, US Ninth Air Force. (US National Archives)

Above: P-51D Mustang 44-14507, of the 364th Fighter Squadron, 357th Fighter Group, USAAF 8th Air Force, lands at Leiston in 1944. The name *Tangerine* refers to a popular song of the time made famous by the Jimmy Dorsey Orchestra. (H Holmes via Andrew Thomas)

Below: Sporting long-range drop tanks, P-51D 44-72710 of the 357th Fighter Group waits on its dispersal for the next mission during the latter stages of World War Two. (USAF Academy via Andrew Thomas)

P-51D Mustang 44-13410 *Lou IV* served with the 8th Air Force's 361st Fighter Group during World War Two. Originally the yellow nose only manifested itself on the spinner and on a 12in (30cm) band on the nose, but later in the war it was stretched almost all the way back to the fighter's windscreen, in order to avoid confusion with yellow-nosed 9th AF P-51s. (Pete West)

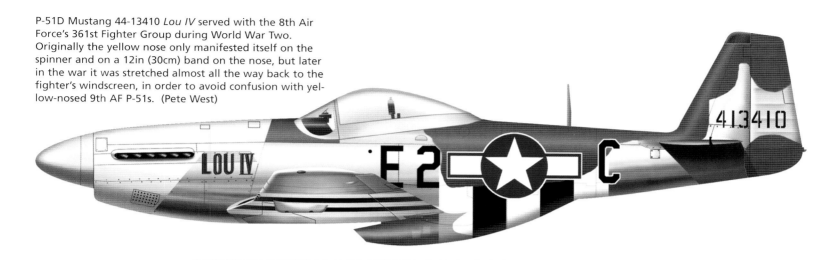

Below: Lt Murphy, pilot of P-51D *Jersey Bouncer,* a Honington-based 364th Fighter Group aircraft, poses with his crew chief on December 20, 1944. (Ken Delve Collection)

363rd FG*	
Squadrons	380th, 381st and 382nd FS
Air Force	9th AF
Aircraft	P-51, F-5, F-6
Operational	Feb 1944 to May 1945
Bases	Keevil, Rivenhall, Staplehurst, UK; Maupertuis, Azeville, Le Mans, France; Luxembourg; Le Culot, Belgium; Venlo, Holland; Gütersloh, Brunswick, Wiesbaden, Germany
	* TRG from Sept 1944

364th FG	
Squadrons	383rd, 384th and 385th FS
Air Force	8th AF
Aircraft	P-38J, P-51D
Operational	Mar 1944 to May 1945
Bases	Honington, UK

479th FG	
Squadrons	434th, 435th and 436th FS
Air Force	8th AF
Aircraft	P-38J/L, P-51D/K
Operational	May 1944 to May 1945
Bases	Wattisham, UK

Royal Air Force	
Unit	**2 Sqn**
Aircraft	Mustang I, Ia, II
Operational	Apr 1942 to Jan 1945
Bases	Sawbridgeworth, Bottisham, Fowlmere, Gravesend, Odiham, North Weald, Dundonald, Gatwick, UK; B.10 Plumetot, B.4 Beny-sur-mer, B.27 Boisney, B.31 Fresnoy Folney, B.43 Fort Rouge, France; B.61 St Denis Westrem, B.70 Deurne, Belgium; B.77 Gilze – Rijen, The Netherlands
Unit	**4 Sqn**
Aircraft	Mustang I
Operational	Apr 1942 to Jan 1944
Bases	Clifton, Barford St John, Cranfield, Duxford, Bottisham, Gravesend, Odiham, Funtington, North Weald, Sawbridgeworth, Aston Down, UK
Unit	**16 Sqn**
Aircraft	Mustang I
Operational	Apr 1942 to Nov 1943
Bases	Weston Zoyland, Thruxton, Lympne, Andover, Middle Wallop, Hartford Bridge, UK
Unit	**19 Sqn**
Aircraft	Mustang III, Mustang IV
Operational	Feb 1944 to Mar 1946
Bases	Gravesend, Ford, Southend, Funtingdon, Ford, UK; B.7 Martragny, B.12 Ellon, B-24 St Andre del 'Eure, B.40 Nivillers, France; B.60 Grimbergen, Belgium; Matlask, Andrews Field, Peterhead, Acklington, Bradwell Bay, Molesworth, UK
Unit	**26 Sqn**
Aircraft	Mustang I
Operational	Jan 1942 to March 1944, December 1944 to June 1945
Bases	Gatwick, Weston Zoyland, Detling, Stoney Cross, East Manton, Red Barn, Martlesham Heath, Ballyhalbert, Church Fenton, Hutton Cranswick, Scorton, Peterhead, Exeter, Harrowbeer, North Weald, Cognac, Chilbolton, UK

Top: A fine view of Mustang I AG550, taken when it was serving with 2 Sqn in the late summer of 1943. The aircraft was ultimately destroyed in a crash (while still serving with 2 Sqn) on May 26, 1945. (2 Sqn via Andrew Thomas)

Above: AG487 'Wilma 1', an Allison-engined Mustang I of 4 Sqn is pictured at Clifton during 1943. (Ken Delve Collection)

Below: Flying Officer D W Sampson (left) adjusts his parachute straps before getting in the cockpit of Allison-engined Mustang I AG431 at Middle Wallop in June 1943. (J D Oughton via Andrew Thomas)

Unit	63 Sqn
Aircraft	Mustang I, Mustang Ia
Operational	Jun 1942 to May 1944
	Bases Gatwick, Catterick, Weston Zoyland, Macmerry, Lossiemouth, Odiham, Dalcross, Acklington, Turnhouse, Thruxton, Sawbridgeworth, North Weald, Benson, Peterhead, Tealing, Dundonald, Ballyhalbert, Woodvale, Lee-on-Solent, UK

Unit	64 Sqn
Aircraft	Mustang III, Mustang IV
Operational	Nov 1944 to Jun 1946
	Bases Bradwell Bay, Bentwaters, Horsham St Faith, UK

Unit	65 Sqn
Aircraft	Mustang III, Mustang IV
Operational	Dec 1943 to May 1946
Bases	Gravesend, Ford, Funtington, B.7 Martragny, B.12 Ellon, B.40 Beauvais, B.60 Grimbergen, Matlask, Andrews Field, Peterhead, Banff, Bentwaters, Hethel, Spilsby, Horsham St Faith, UK

Unit	93 Sqn
Aircraft	Mustang III, Mustang IV
Operational	Jan 1946 to Dec 1946
Bases	Lavariano, Tissano, Treviso, Italy

Unit	112 Sqn
Aircraft	Mustang III, Mustang IV
Operational	June 1944 to Dec 1946
Bases	San Angelo, Guidonia, Falerium, Crete, Iesi, Fano, Cervia, Lavariano, Treviso, Italy

Top: With its groundcrew team giving the Rolls Royce Merlin some attention, Mustang III FZ190 is prepared for the next sortie at B.12 Ellon airfield in France during August 1944. (19 Sqn Archives via Andrew Thomas)

Above: 26 Sqn operated Allison-engined Mustang Is up until the end of World War Two. AM148 is pictured during 1943 and shows the distinctive upper cowling air intake, one of the early Mustang's recognition features. (26 Sqn via Andrew Thomas)

Below: Although retaining the famed North American design throughout the war, by March 1945 26 Sqn had changed its unit codes, replacing RM with XC, as can be seen from this March 1945 Mustang I duo. (26 Sqn via Andrew Thomas)

Bottom: With the majority of the aircraft in this line-up still sporting the distinctive sharkmouth nose-art (a left-over from the days when the squadron operated Curtiss P-40 Kittyhawks), these Mustang IVs of 112 Sqn are pictured at Treviso, Italy, in 1946. (R A Brown via Andrew Thomas)

Below: Wg Cdr Max Sutherland (Wg Cdr flying) and Sqn Ldr Tony Drew (Officer Commanding) (L & R respectively) stand in front of this 118 Sqn Mustang III at Bentwaters in 1945, which, although it wears the unit's NK-O codes, does not bear an RAF serial number! Note the natural metal finish and 'Malcolm-hooded' cockpit canopy. (D McCaig via Andrew Thomas)

Unit	118 Sqn
Aircraft	Mustang III, Mustang IV
Operational	Jan 1945 to Mar 1946
Bases	Bentwaters, Fairwood Common, Horsham St Faith, UK

Unit	122 Sqn
Aircraft	Mustang III, Mustang IV
Operational	Feb 1944 to Aug 1945
Bases	Gravesend, Ford, Funtington, Southend, UK; B.7 Martragny, B.12 Ellon, B.24 St Andre de l'Eure, B.42 Beauvais/Tille, France; B.60 Grimbergen, Belgium; Matlask, Andrews Field, Peterhead, Dyce, UK

Unit	126 Sqn
Aircraft	Mustang III, Mustang IV
Operational	Dec 1944 to Mar 1946
Bases	Bradwell Bay, Bentwaters, Hethel, UK

Unit	129 Sqn
Aircraft	Mustang III
Operational	Apl 1944 to May 1945
Bases	Coolham, Holmsley South, Brenzett, Andrews Field, Bentwaters, UK

Unit	154 Sqn
Aircraft	Mustang IV
Operational	Feb 1945 to Mar 1945
Bases	Biggin Hill, Hunsdon, UK

Unit	165 Sqn
Aircraft	Mustang III
Operational	Feb 1945 to Jun 1945
Bases	Bentwaters, Dyce, UK

Unit	168 Sqn
Aircraft	Mustang I, Mustang Ia
Operational	Nov 1942 to Oct 1944
Bases	Odiham, Weston Zoyland, Hutton Cranswick Huggate, Thruxton, Sawbridgeworth, North Weald, Llanbedr, Gatwick, , UK; B.8 Sommervieu, B.21 St Honorine, B.34 Avrilly, France; B.64 Shaffen Diest, Belgium; B.78 Eindhoven, The Netherlands

Unit	169 Sqn
Aircraft	Mustang I
Operational	Jun 1942 to Sept 1943
Bases	Twinwood Farm, Doncaster, Weston Zoyland, Clifton, Duxford, Barford St John, Gransden Lodge, Bottisham, Andover, Middle Wallop, UK.

Unit	170 Sqn
Aircraft	Mustang I, Mustang Ia
Operational	Jun 1942 to Jan 1944
Bases	Weston Zoyland, Hurn, Thruxton, Andover, Ford, Snailwell, Odiham, UK

Unit	171 Sqn
Aircraft	Mustang Ia
Operational	Sept 1942 to Dec 1942
Bases	Gatwick, Weston Zoyland, Hartfordbridge, UK

Centre left: A formation of cannon-armed Mustang IAs of 170 Sqn fly across the English landscape in September 1943. (D Clarke via Andrew Thomas)

Left: Complete with 'D Day' stripes on the wings and fuselage, two Mustangs of 168 Sqn wait in readiness for the next sortie, while their pilots take a well-earned rest between operations 'somewhere in Europe'. (Ken Delve Collection)

Unit	213 Sqn
Aircraft	Mustang III, Mustang IV
Operational	May 1944 to Feb 1947
Bases	Idku, Egypt; Leverano, Biferno, Italy; Prkos, Yugoslavia; Brindisi, Italy; Ramat David, Palestine; Nicosia, Cyprus

Unit	225 Sqn
Aircraft	Mustang I, Mustang II
Operational	May 1942 to Aug 1943
Bases	Abbotsinch, Thruxton, Macmerry, UK; Maison Blanche, Bone, Souk-el-Arba, Algeria; Arjana, Bou Ficha, Tunisia

Unit	231 Sqn
Aircraft	Mustang I
Operational	Apr 1943 to Jan 1944
Bases	York, Dunsfold, Weston Zoyland, Woodchurch, Redhill, UK

Unit	234 Sqn
Aircraft	Mustang III, Mustang IV
Operational	Sept 1944 to Aug 1945
Bases	Bentwaters, Peterhead, Dyce, UK

Unit	239 Sqn
Aircraft	Mustang I
Operational	May 1942 to Sept 1943
Bases	Gatwick, Twinwood Farm, Cranfield, Odiham, Hurn, Stoney Cross, Fairlop, Martlesham Heath, Hornchurch, UK

Unit	241 Sqn
Aircraft	Mustang I
Operational	Mar 1942 to Nov 1942
Bases	Bottisham, Ayr, UK; Maison Blanche, Algeria

Unit	249 Sqn
Aircraft	Mustang III, Mustang IV
Operational	Sep 1944 to Aug 1945
Bases	Canne, Italy; Prkos, Yugoslavia; Biferno, Brindisi, Italy

Unit	250 Sqn
Aircraft	Mustang III, Mustang IV
Operational	Aug 1945 to Jan 1947
Bases	Lavariano, Tissano, Treviso, Italy

Top: This 213 Sqn Mustang III sports the sign of the Unicorn public house on its fuselage side. For May and June of 1945 the unit was based at Biferno airfield in Italy. 213 Sqn records via Andrew Thomas)

Above: Mustang IV KH761 saw service with 213 Sqn and is pictured here in Nicosia during 1945. (Andrew Thomas Collection)

Below: KH568, a Mustang III of 249 Sqn hit a hole in the runway during take off at Biferno, Italy, on November 12, 1944, writing off the undercarriage, propeller and radiator scoop in the process. Its pilot, who looks relieved to have survived the incident, stands on the wing root. Note the unusual presentation of the unit's GN-H code letters. (J Te Kloot via Andrew Thomas)

Unit	260 Sqn
Aircraft	Mustang III, Mustang IV
Operational	Apr 1944 to Aug 1945
Bases	Cutella, San Angelo, Guidonia, Falerium, Crete, Iesi, Fano, Cervia, Lavariano, Italy

Unit	268 Sqn
Aircraft	Mustang I, Mustang Ia, Mustang II
Operational	Mar 1942 to Aug 1945
Bases	Ibsley, Weston Zoyland, Snailwell, Wing, Bottisham, Odiham, Tangmere, Funtington, Thruxton, Turnhouse, North Weald, Llanbedr, Sawbridgeworth, Dundonald, Gatwick, UK; B.10 Plumetot, B.4 Beny-sur-Mer, B.27 Boisney, B.31 Fresnoy Folny, B.43 Fort Rouge, France; B.61 St Denia Westrem, B.70 Deurne, Belgium; B.77 Gilze-Rijen, The Netherlands; Fairwood Common, UK; B.77 Gilze-Rijen, B.89 Mill, B.106 Twente, The Netherlands; B.118 Celle, B.150 Hustedt, Germany

Unit	285 Sqn
Aircraft	Mustang I
Operational	Mar 1945 to Jun 1945
Bases	North Weald, Weston Zoyland, UK

Unit	303 Sqn
Aircraft	Mustang IV
Operational	Apr 1945 to Dec 1946
Bases	Andrews Field, Turnhouse, Wick, Charterhall, Hethel, UK

Unit	306 Sqn
Aircraft	Mustang III
Operational	Mar 1944 to Jan 1947
Bases	Heston, Coolham, Holmsley South, Ford, Brenzett, Andrews Field, Coltishall, Fairwood Common, UK

Unit	309 Sqn
Aircraft	Mustang III, Mustang IV
Operational	Oct 1944 to Jan 1947
Bases	Peterhead, Andrews Field, Coltishall, Bradwell Bay, UK

Unit	315 Sqn
Aircraft	Mustang III
Operational	Mar 1944 to Dec 1946
Bases	Heston, Coolham, Holmsley South, Ford, Brenzett, Andrews Field, Coltishall, Fairwood Common, UK

Unit	316 Sqn
Aircraft	Mustang III
Operational	Apr 1944 to Nov 1946
Bases	Bases Coltishall, West Malling, Friston, Andrews Field, Fairwood Common, Wick, Hethel, UK

Unit	516 Sqn
Aircraft	Mustang I
Bases	Operational Apr 1943 to Feb 1944 Dundonald, UK

Unit	541 Sqn
Aircraft	Mustang III
Operational	Jun 1944 to Apr 1945
Bases	Benson, UK

Unit	611 Sqn
Aircraft	Mustang IV
Operational	Jan 1945 to Aug 1945
Bases	Hawkinge, Hunsdon, Peterhead, UK

Unit	613 Sqn
Aircraft	Mustang I
Operational	Apr 1942 to Oct 1943
Bases	Twinwood Farm, Ouston, Wing, Bottisham, Ringway, Wellingore, Clifton, Portreath, Snailwell, Lasham, UK

In addition to the standard use of Mustangs in the operational squadrons of the RAF, Bomber Command's 617 Squadron (the famed 'Dambusters unit) also operated a small number of Mustangs. In the years following the Dams raid, Wing Commander Leonard Cheshire, by then the unit's Commanding Officer, pioneered the radical use of Mustang fighters as target marking aircraft.

P-51s were also used by a wide range of other RAF units, including: 61 Operational Training Unit (OUT), 71 OUT, 236 OUT, 1 Armament Practice School, 1 Tactical Exercise Unit (TEU), 3 TEU, 5 Refresher Flying Unit, Aeroplane and Armament Experimental Establishment, Central Fighter Establishment, Central Gunnery School, Fighter Interception Unit, Fighter Interceptor Development Unit and the Royal Aircraft Establishment.

Below: A pair of rocket-equipped 250 Sqn Mustang IIIs await the next sortie at their Treviso base in Italy. (W/C A G Todd via Andrew Thomas)

Bottom: It's unsure whether this particular Mustang IV, KM263, PD-T of 303 Sqn is receiving major work to the air-frame or is in the process of being scrapped. The photograph was taken in 1946, right at the end of the unit's association with the P-51. (J D Oughton via Andrew Thomas)

Royal Australian Air Force

The Commonwealth Aircraft Factory in Australia licence-built Mustangs, after assembling 80 from parts supplied by the USA, which were designated as CA-17 Mustang 20s. A further 120 would be constructed using Australian-built components. 14, built initially as Mk 21s, would be upgraded to Mk 22 standard. A batch of 26 Mk 21s was followed by 67 Mk 23s, with a final order for 13 Mk 22 tactical reconnaissance aircraft bringing up the rear in terms of Australian-built machines.

Unit	3 Sqn
Aircraft	Mustang III, Mustang IV
Operational	Nov 1944 to Aug 1945
Bases	Fano, Cervia, Lavariano, Italy

Unit	450 Sqn
Aircraft	Mustang III
Operational	May 1945 to Aug 1945
Bases	Lavariano, Italy

Right: A68-171 is typical of the Australian-built Mustangs, the aircraft wearing no camouflage as such, just national insignia. '171 was obviously a well-used aircraft, judging by the oil and coolant stains running down the fuse-lage. (Key Collection)

Middle: 78 Sqn RAAF flew A68-71 post World War Two, as this 1946 photo-graph illustrates. Note the small Commonwealth Aircraft Corporation trade-mark stencil on the rudder, as HU-A taxies out from its dispersal. (RAAF via Andrew Thomas)

Below: This former RAAF Mustang IV, A68-113, ended its flying days in 1957 as a target tug air-craft. (J W Bennett via Andrew Thomas)

Left: Photographed at RAF Digby in June 1945, eight Mustang IVs of 442 Sqn, complete with drop tanks, are lined up on the grass. (A J Malladaine via Andrew Thomas)

Centre left: In the 1950s 402 Sqn RCAF operated P-51D Mustangs. AC-297 basks in the sun at Stevenson Field, Manitoba. (J McNulty via Andrew Thomas)

Bottom: One of the Mustangs in the line-up at Digby was KH680 Y2-B, which wears its individual aircraft letter B below the windscreen instead of on the rear fuselage. The aircraft at rest on the grass, with attendant fuel bowser in the background, makes for a somewhat pastoral scene, quite divorced from the daily terrors of war! A J Malladaine via Andrew Thomas)

Royal Canadian Air Force

Unit	400 Sqn
Aircraft	Mustang I
Operational	Apl 1942 to Feb 1944
Bases	Gatwick, Odiham, Middle Wallop, Dunsfold, UK

Unit	414 Sqn
Aircraft	Mustang I
Operational	Jun 1942 to Aug 1944
Bases	Abbotsinch, Dunsfold, Middle Wallop, Harrowbeer, Portreath, Gatwick, Weston Zoyland, Ashford, Woodchurch, Redhill, Peterhead, Odiham, Dundonald, UK

Unit	430 Sqn
Aircraft	Mustang I
Operational	Jan 1943 to Jan 1945
Bases	Hartfordbridge, Dunsfold, Gatwick, Ashford, Clifton, Odiham, UK; France; B.8 Sommervieu, B.21 St Honorine, B.34 Evreux/Avrilly, B.66 Diest, Belgium; B.78 Eindhoven, The Netherlands

Unit	441 Sqn
Aircraft	Mustang III, Mustang IV
Operational	May 1945 to Aug 1945
Bases	Digby, Molesworth, UK

Unit	442 Sqn
Aircraft	Mustang IV
Operational	Mar 1945 to Aug 1945
Bases	Hunsdon, Digby, Molesworth, UK

South African Air Force

Unit	1 Sqn
Aircraft	Mustang III, Mustang IV
Operational	Jun 1945 to Jul 1945
Bases	Lavariano, Italy

Unit	2 Sqn
Aircraft	Mustang IV
Operational	Jun 1945 to Jul 1945
Bases	Tissano, Italy

Unit	5 Sqn
Aircraft	Mustang III, Mustang IV
Operational	Sept 1944 to Oct 1945
Bases	Iesi, Fano, Cervia, Lavariano, Italy

Right: Coded GL-N, this Mustang IV of 5 Sqn SAAF is pictured at the point of touch down at Fano airfield in Italy during 1945. (F F Smith via Andrew Thomas)

Below: After operating Mustang IVs until the end of World War Two, 2 Sqn SAAF continued to use P-51D variants into the 1950s, as this illustration of 335 taken at K-46 Hoengsong airfield in mid-1951 shows. The aircraft is well-equipped for action with both rockets and bombs slung under the wings. (SAAF via Andrew Thomas)

Below: F-51D Mustang 335 of 2 Sqn (Flying Cheetahs) SAAF, based at Pyongyang East when it was operating as part of the 18th Fighter Bomber Wing of the USAF in December 1950. (Pete West)

Above: Dick Thurman's Mustang wears the markings of 44-14812 *Slender, Tender & Tall*, whereas the airframe's real identity is 44-74950, which was one of a batch of 800 P-51D-10NA aircraft built by North American Aviation Inc. (Key – Duncan Cubitt)

Below: P-51C 42-103645 (NL61429) operated by the Texas-based Commemorative Air Force.

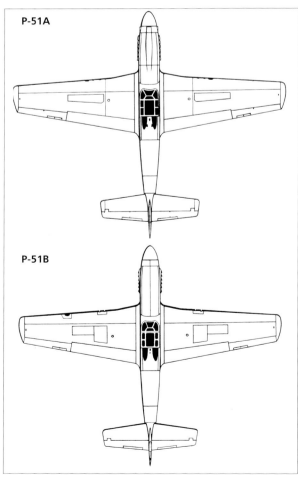

NORTH AMERICAN P-51 PRODUCTION				
Model	**NA design**	**Serials**	**C/n**	**Quantity**
NA-73X	73X	(I)	73-3097	1
Mustang 1	73	AG345/664 (for RAF)	73-3098/3100, 73-3102/3106, 73-3108/3416, 73-4767/4768, 73-7812	320
XP-51	73	41-038/039	73-3101 & 3107	2
Mustang I	83	AL958/999, AM100/257, AP164/263 (for RAF)	83-4769/5068	300
P-51-NA	91	41-37320/37351, 41-37353/37420, 41-37422/37469	91-11981/12130	148
P-51A-1NA	99	43-6003/6102	99-22106/22205	100
P-51A-5NA	99	43-6103/6157	99-22206/22260	55
P-51C-1NA	99	43-6158/6312	99-22261/22415	155
XP-51B	101	41-37352, 41-37421 (from P-51-NA order)		
P-51B-1NA	102	43-12093/12492	102-24541/24940	400
P-51B-5NA	104	43-6313/652 43-6353/6752 43-6753/7112	104-24501/24540 104-24941/25340 104-25343/25702	800
P-51B-10NA	104	43-7113/7202 42-106429/106538 42-106541/106738	104-25703/25792 104-22816/22925 104-22928/23125	398
P-51B-I5NA	104	42-106739/106978 43-24752/24901	104-23126/23305 104-25781/25930	390
P-51C-1NT	103	42-102979/103328	103-22416/22765	350
P-51C-5NT	103	42-103329/103378 42-103379/103778	103-27766/22815 103-25933/26332	50 400
P-51C-10NT	103	42-103779/103978 43-24902/25251	103-103-26333/26532 103-26533/26882	200 350
	111	44-10753/10782	111-28886/28915	30
P-51C-11NT	111	44-10783/10817	111-28916/28950	35
P-51C-10NT	111	44-10818/10852	111-28951/28995	35
P-51C-11NT	111	44-10853/10858	111-28996/29001	6
P-51C-10NT	111	44-10859/11036	111-29002/29179	178
P-51C-11NT	111	44-11037/11122	111-29180/29255	86
P-51C-10NT	111	44-11123/11152	111-29256/29285	30
XP-51D-NA	106	42-106539/106540	106-25341/25342	2
P-51D-5NA	109	44-13253/14052	109-26886/27685	800
P-51D-10NA	109	44-14053/14852	109-27686/28485	800
P-51D-15NA	109	44—14853/15252 44-15253/15752	109-28486/28885 109-35536/36035	900 500

NORTH AMERICAN P-51 PRODUCTION CONTINUED				
P-51D-1NA	110	To Australia Unassembled	110-34386/34485	100
P-51D-20NA	122	44-63160/64159	122-30886/31885	1000
		44-72027/72126	122-31886/31985	100
		44-72127/72626	122-38586/39085	500
P-51D-25NA	122	44-72627/73626	122-39086/40085	1000
		44-73627/74226	122-40167/40766	600
P-51D-30NA	122	44-74227/75026	122-40767/41566	800
P-51D-5NT	111	44-11153/11352	111-29286/29485	200
P-51D-20NT	111	44-12853/13252	111-36136/36535	400
P-51D-25NT	124	44-84390/84989 (44-84610/84611 built as TP-51D)	124-44246/44845	600
		45-11343/11542	124-48096/48295	200
P-51D-30NT	124	45-11543/11742 (45-11443/11450 built as TP-51D)	124-48296/48495	200
XP-51F	105	43-43332/43334	105-26883/26885	3
XP-51G	105	43-43335/43336	105-25931/25932	2
XP-51J	105	44-76027/76028	105-47446/47447	2
P-51H-1NA	126	44-64160/64179	126-37586/37605	20
P-51H-5NA	126	44-64180/64459	126-37606/37885	280
P-51H-10NA	126	44-64460/64714	126-37886/38140	255
P-51K-1NT	111	44-11353/11552	111-29486/29685	200
P-51K-5NT	111	44-11553/11952	111-29686/30085	400
P-51K-10NT	111	44-11953/12752	111-30086/30885	800
	111	44-12753/12852	111-36036/36135	100
P-51M-1NT	124	45-11743	124-48496	1
A-36A-NA	97	42-83663/84162	97-15581/16380	500
XP-82NA	120	44-83886/83887	120-43742/43743	2
XP-82A-NA	120	44-83888	120-43744	1
P-82B-NA	123	44-65160/65179	123-43746/43765	20
P-82C-NA	123	44-65169	(converted from P-82B)	1
P-82D-NA	123	44-65170	(converted from P-82B)	1
P-82E-NA	144	46-0255/0354	144-38141/38240	100
P-82F-NA	149	46-0405/0504 (0469/0504 built as P-82H then converted to G)	149-38291/38390	100
P-82G-NA	150	46-0355/0404	150-38241/38290	50
F-51D Cavalier			67-14862/14865	4
		(Sold to Bolivia)		
		67-22579/22582		4
		(Sold to Bolivia)		
		68-15795/15796		2
TF-51D		67-14866		1
		(Sold to Bolivia)		

The F-6 designation was given to photo-reconnaissance Mustangs that were built as such among the P-51 production runs. Approximately 126 early Mustangs were converted to F-6B and F-6C, while F-6D and F-6K conversions were: F-6D-20NT 44-13020/l3039, 44-13131/13140, 44-13181; F-6D-25NT 44-84509/84540, 44-84566, 44-84773/84778, 44-84835/84855; F-6K-5NT 44-11554, 44-11897/11952; F-6K-10NT 44-11993/12008, 44-12216/12237, 44-12459/12471, 44-12523/12534; F-6K-15NT 44-12810/12852. The A-36A designation applied to aircraft that were designed purely for ground attack duties. As well as those built as TP-5/Ds, the following were also modified to TF-51Ds 44-84654/84658, 44-84660, 44-84662/84663, 44-84665/84670, 44-84676. The F-51 Cavalier Mustangs were produced from re-worked P 51D airframes. (Production list compiled by Mark Nicholls)

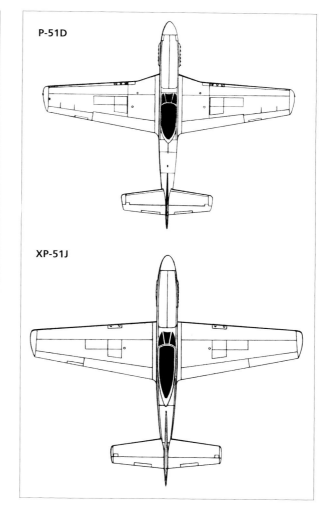

P-51D

XP-51J

Above: CA-18 Mustang A68-100 (N51AB) owned and flown by California-based Brian Adams.

Below: Mustang 44-13964 was one of a batch of 800 P-51D-5NA variants built by North American Aviation Inc, which ran from 44-13253 to 44-14052. (Pete West)

THE WORLD'S SURVIVING MUSTANGS

Today's airworthy Mustangs all have varied backgrounds and service histories. Some are genuine World War Two veterans which have seen action on a number of fronts, while other restorations are what amounts to a compendium of different airframes and parts put together to create a complete P-51. That latter statement is not intended to denigrate any of the restorer's work in this field, but rather to highlight the fact that some aircraft have historical provenance, while others may not have such an illustrious past in their log books.

Nevertheless, readers of this book will probably all admit to getting a thrill when watching a Mustang being put through its paces at an airshow. When witnessing this spectacle, one tends not to think of the individual history behind the aircraft, being more intent in soaking up the sight and sound of the P-51 in its natural element.

In this chapter we look at a random selection of 15 surviving Mustangs around the globe, and chart their histories, such as they are. Following these histories is a directory of the world's population of surviving airframes, which has been compiled from a number of sources.

HOLLAND
P-51D 44-74425 (NL11T) *Damn Yankee*
Tom van der Meulen/Dutch Mustang Flight, Lelystad
This aircraft is one of the examples, which passed through the hands of James Defurias and Fred Ritts of Intercontinental Airways during the late 1950s. At that time it was registered as N6522D. Prior to that it served with the Royal Canadian Air Force as RCAF 9591 from 1950 until 1958. Having had nine private owners during the late 1950s and 1960s, the Mustang ended up with warbird collector Harold Bubba Beal of Concord, Tennessee. The fighter suffered some damage on landing during October 1972 and after repair was sold on to John Herlihy of Half Moon Bay in California, who re-registered it as N11T. John raced the aircraft using the race #8... that was until a taxiing accident at home base on November 19, 1974, grounded the P-51 again.

Moving on through four more owners, the Mustang was damaged once more during a forced landing in October 1982 while in the ownership of Gordon Plaskett. Further repairs to the airframe had to be carried out, after which it worked its way through six more private owners!

After a period in the ownership of Bob Pond's Planes of Fame East, the aircraft was resident during early 1994 with the Western Aviation Maintenance facility at Mesa, Arizona, which was preparing the Mustang for a long transatlantic flight. The fighter had been acquired by the Dutch Mustang Flight in Lelystad and had already started to accumulate European airshow bookings. *Damn Yankee* made its UK display debut in the D-Day Plus 50 segment of Mildenhall's Air Fete in 1994. Since then it has made occasional appearances at British airshows, with Duxford and Wroughton events springing to mind.

NEW ZEALAND
P-51D 44-73420 (ZK-PLI) *Miss Torque*
Alpine Fighter Collection, Wanaka
A Mustang with a colourful history, 44-73420 was built at North American's Inglewood factory and was initially put on board a ship bound for the Middle East in April 1945. However, the ship returned to America with the P-51 still on board and the fighter was flown to Olmstead Air Base,

Below: Even though its home base is in Holland, 44-74425 (NL11T) *Damn Yankee* has made a number of airshow appearances in the UK. It is seen here landing during the 1994 Great Warbirds Air Display at Wroughton. (Key – Steve Fletcher)

Bottom: Taxying out during a Confederate Air Force Airsho at Harlingen, Texas, USA, while in the ownership of Robb Satterfield, this particular Mustang is now operated in New Zealand by the Alpine Fighter Collection at Wanaka. (Key - Duncan Cubitt)

Left: *From the pilot's seat.* Alister Kay pilots the Old Flying Machine Company's P-51D, bringing up the rear in the box of four fighters (l to r: Spitfire, Corsair and P-40) as the Breitling Fighters Team approach Buochs in Switzerland during September 2001. (Key – Duncan Cubitt)

Lower right: For a couple of seasons in the late 1990s this Mustang shed its *Old Crow* markings for a very colourful *Detroit Miss* set of colours. At the time of this book's compilation N167F had reverted to its former 357th Fighter Group hue. (Key – Robert J Rudhall)

Below: Captured in a typical Duxford setting, P-51C 43-25147 (G-PSIC) *Princess Elizabeth* runs its Merlin engine before performing at the October airshow in 1997. (Key - Robert J Rudhall)

Below right: On finals to land at Duxford in 1991, Mustang 44-63507 (NL51EA) *Double Trouble Two* is based at Basle in Switzerland with Max Vogelsang/Swiss Warbirds. (Key - Duncan Cubitt)

Pasadena, for modifications. In 1947 the Mustang was issued to the Air National Guard and served with a number of ANG units before being retired from active service in 1958.

Passing through six civilian owners, the fighter eventually ended up in the ownership of Aaron Giebel, Robb Satterfield and Dallas Smith at Harlingen, Texas, in 1978. Before this trio took possession of the aircraft it had been used as an aerial platform for weapons which were being developed for use in the Vietnam War!

Overhauled and given the nickname *Miss Torque,* the aircraft was flown at airshows in the USA for a number of years until it was acquired by Brian Hore and Tim Wallis of The Alpine Fighter Collection in New Zealand. During December 1993 the Mustang was shipped to its new home at Wanaka, reassembled and flight tested in time to take part in the Warbirds over Wanaka Airshow the following year. Now registered as ZK-PLI the P-51D retains its *Miss Torque* colours and markings.

NORWAY
P-51D 44-73877 (N167F) *Old Crow*
Scandinavian Historic Flight, Oslo

One of the regular airshow performers in Europe, the Scandinavian Historic Flight's (SHF) *Old Crow* was built and delivered to the USAAF in 1944. Seeing no operational service, it spent most of its wartime career on the strength of US-based training units, before being transferred to the Royal Canadian Air Force in 1951. The aircraft spent seven years with the Canadians before being struck off charge in April 1958.

During the 1960s, 1970s and early 1980s the Mustang was operated by a succession of private owners in Canada and the USA, before being grounded for a major overhaul in the hands of RLS 51 Limited. The aircraft was stripped right down to the bare bones, skinning was replaced on the tailcone along with some areas on the wings and cowling fairings, lightweight foam-filled fuel tanks were inserted into the wings, a baggage door was fitted to the port fuselage side and the cockpit was completely furnished in leather upholstery. Instrumentation included a three-axis autopilot and a fully updated avionics suite. Hovey Machine Products rebuilt the Merlin engine and the aircraft was given a new colour scheme, which represented *Old Crow*, the example flown by Chuck Yeager's wingman Captain Bud Anderson of the 357th Fighter Group.

Old Crow flew across the Atlantic in June 1986, joining the SHF in Norway, after performing at a number of

UK airshows. Operated out of Oslo by SHF, *Old Crow* took part in the filming of the motion picture *Memphis Belle* in 1989, and can be seen at UK airshows during the summer months on a regular basis.

SWITZERLAND
P-51D 44-63507 (NL51EA) *Double Trouble Two*
Max Vogelsang/Swiss Warbirds, Basle

Currently the only airworthy Mustang in Switzerland, this former Royal Canadian Air Force machine was 'demobbed' in 1947 and since then has gone through a multitude of civilian owners. It was first purchased by two Intercontinental Airways pilots, James Defurias and Fred Ritts, as N6345T, who operated it from 1957 to 1960. It was then acquired by Aero Enterprises, which passed it on to Harold Hacker.

After a landing accident in February 1964, the fighter returned to Aero Enterprises, was repaired and by 1965 was owned by Gardner Flyers Inc at Brownwood in Texas. Another accident badly damaged the Mustang and it had to be rebuilt yet again, this time by Ray Stutsman.

On completion of the rebuild, the Mustang was sold to Don Davidson who had it painted in the markings of *Double Trouble,* as flown by P-51 ace, Lt Col William Bailey of the 352nd Fighter Squadron. After a few years in these markings, Davidson decided to repaint the aircraft as *Double Trouble Two,* the second Mustang flown by William Bailey.

The aircraft was carrying these new colours when it was acquired by its current owner and flown to Switzerland in 1990. To date, it has only appeared once

in the UK (1991's Classic Fighter Display at Duxford) since coming crossing the Atlantic for its European home.

UNITED KINGDOM
P-51C 43-25147 (G-PSIC) *Princess Elizabeth*
The Fighter Collection, Duxford

This Mustang is currently the only example of a 'razor-back' P-51 in Europe, having been imported from the USA in July of 1997. The aircraft is very much a hybrid machine, and was restored using the tailplane of a P-51B, the fuselage of a P-51D and the mainplane of a P-51B, by Pete Regina in the USA during the late 1970s and early 1980s.

Regina discovered a complete P-51B wing lying in a yard behind a technical school in Israel during the late 1970s, and along with the other aforementioned portions of Mustang, set about building a complete P-51. The fuselage was constructed by building up a P-51D rear fuselage into the 'razorback' shape of the earlier Mustang marks, using plaster casts taken from an extant P-51C owned by warbird collector and film flyer Frank Tallman.

After many hours of work, the P-51 was ready to take to the air again and Dave Zeuschel piloted the fighter on its first post-restoration flight on June 11, 1981. Pete Regina kept the aircraft for five years before selling it on to Joe Kasperoff in 1986, who in turn sold it to The Fighter Collection (TFC) in 1996. On arrival in the UK, the P-51C was assembled in record time, painted in the markings of P-51B 42-106449 *Princess Elizabeth,* of the 487th Fighter Squadron, 352nd Fighter Group, US 8th Air Force, and debuted at the 1997 Flying Legends Airshow at Duxford on July 12/13.

With its 'high back' configuration, G-PSIC makes an ideal stablemate for TFC's recently acquired 'low back' P-51D G-CBNM.

P-51D 44-63864 (G-CBNM)
The Fighter Collection, Duxford, UK.

This Mustang has served with a number of different air arms — the Swedes, the Italians and the Israelis. At some time in its life it adopted the identity of 44-63864, which had been built at Inglewood and taken on charge by the US Army Air Force in December 1944. In the early part of 1945 it was shipped to the UK and served with the Duxford-based 78th Fighter Group. Wearing the nose-art *Twilight Tear,* the P-51 is credited with three 'kills' including two Messerschmitt 262 jet fighters! Postwar it was purchased by the Swedish Government and ferried to Sweden via Scotland. It is at this point that the aircraft's identity becomes cloudy, as some sources have it serving with the Swedes and then passing on to the Italian Air Force, before ending up in Israel. However, it is known that the Mustang was stored at the Israeli Defence Air Force's museum at Herzlia during the mid-1970s.

In 1978 former IDF pilot Israel Itzhaki purchased what remained of the fighter and began to restore it to flying condition. Aided by Peter and Angelo Regina, as well as David Zeuschel in the USA, the aircraft slowly took shape and flew again, registered as 4X-AIM, on February 5, 1984. The aircraft flew only occasionally in Itzhaki's ownership and in 1986 it was decided to sell it. Acquired by Leif Jaraker at Malmo in Sweden, the Mustang was ferried to its new home during December 1986.

Put back into full Swedish Air Force markings, as Fv26158/K, the aircraft was active on the European airshow circuit, and during 1994/96 was put on loan to the Netherlands-based Duke of Brabant Air Force. During the Spring of 2002 The Fighter Collection at Duxford purchased the Mustang and the aircraft returned to its former 78th Fighter Group home on April 5 to fly alongside TFC's other historic warbirds. In the fullness of time it is hoped that the Mustang will re-appear on the UK airshow circuit in its authentic 78th FG markings as *Twilight Tear.*

P-51D 44-73149 (G-BTCD) *Ferocious Frankie*
Old Flying Machine Company, Duxford

Making its first appearance in the UK at the Biggin Hill International Air Fair of 1981, this P-51D has since become a stalwart of the European display circuit. Built in 1945, the aircraft was allocated to the 8th Air Force in the UK, arriving via Liverpool Docks. The Mustang's stay in the UK was short, only spanning some 11 months, during which time it served at Leiston, Suffolk, among other places. Returning to the USA in January 1946 it was put

Above: Pictured on finals to land at Duxford, the former Swedish-based P-51D had only made this one appearance in the UK since it was imported to Sweden in 1986. The 'combat veteran' now resides in Great Britain with The Fighter Collection. (Key - Duncan Cubitt)

Below: Pictured taking off from Duxford's grass runway for a training sortie in May 2002, the OFMC's P-51D has been active in the UK since it was imported from the USA by The Fighter Collection in 1980. (Key – Duncan Cubitt)

Above; Pictured at the 1994 Reno Air Races, where the fighter formed part of the extensive static display, the Planes of Fame's P-51A has been air-worthy since 1981. (Key - Duncan Cubitt)

Opposite page, bottom: Rob Davies brings *Big Beautiful Doll* in for a landing during the 1999 Flying Legends Airshow. During the summer display season the *Doll* can often be seen in company with Maurice Hammond's immaculately restored P-51D *Janie*. (Key – Duncan Cubitt)

Below: The 2002 Reno Air Races were (reportedly) the last time that *Tiger* Destefani would be seen at the helm of *Strega*. Only time will tell if that statement will become true or false! Here, the racer is towed back to the pit area after springing an oil leak. (Key – Duncan Cubitt)

into storage for a while before being transferred to the Royal Canadian Air Force in June 1947 as 9568.

In 1957 it was sold onto the civilian market and was acquired by James Defurias and Fred Ritts of Intercontinental Airways as N6340T. After being sold during the 1970s to Charles Beck and Edward Modes of Burbank. California, the fighter was painted in an all-red colour scheme, given the name *Candyman* and used for air racing as #7.

In 1976 the fighter changed hands again, being was sold to Dr Robert MacFarlane who only flew it occasionally — after four years ownership was transferred to The Fighter Collection (TFC) at Duxford, Cambs, UK. Flown across the Atlantic, still in its racing colours, by John Crocker, it was repainted into authentic 362nd Fighter Squadron US 8th Air Force markings as '44-63221' G4-S *Moose* at Heathrow Airport in April 1981. Its registration was changed for a short while to N51JJ, before it was put onto the British Civil Aircraft Register as G-BTCD. Like several other UK-based Mustangs it enjoyed a bout of film 'stardom' in *Empire of the Sun* and *Memphis Belle*. Undergoing a complete overhaul after the *Memphis Belle* filming, the airframe was found to be in remarkably good condition, and *Candyman* continued to fly with TFC at airshows throughout Europe.

In 1999 the Mustang was acquired by the Old Flying Machine Company and it now wears the markings of the aircraft flown by Wallace E Hopkins when he served with the 374th Fighter Squadron, 361st Fighter Group, 8th Air Force, during World War Two. The nose-art *Ferocious Frankie,* in honour of Hopkins' wife Frankie is faithfully reproduced on the port nose cowling and the OFMC's P-51D now played a major part in the famed Breitling Fighters Team

CA-18 Mustang 22 A68-192 (G-HAEC) *Big Beautiful Doll*

Rob Davies, Woodchurch, UK

One of the most well-known Mustangs in the UK, this aircraft formed part of the Old Flying Machine Company's (OFMC) fleet of historic warbirds until 1996 when it was sold to its present owner. An Australian-built example of the P-51D, it was constructed by the Commonwealth Aircraft Corporation in 1951 and spent its whole military career based at RAAF Tocumwal. 'Demobbed' in April 1958, it was sold to Chris Braund, who registered the fighter as VH-FCB.

After passing through a couple more private owners, the Mustang was acquired by Protino Inc of Manilla in 1969. Shipped out to its new home, it was then registered as PI-C-651. 1973 saw the fighter heavily damaged in a crash landing at Manilla Airport, after which it was stored in a hangar until being acquired by Ray Hanna and Mal Rose of the Hong Kong Engineering Company (HAEC).

A full rebuild to flying condition was undertaken and the Mustang flew again in February 1985, after which it was dismantled and shipped to the UK, where it joined the OFMC at Duxford. During its time with OFMC it 'starred' in several screen productions — including *Empire of the Sun* and *Memphis Belle* — as well as becoming one of the regular airshow attendees in Europe. Maintained in its Duxford-based 78th Fighter Group *Big Beautiful Doll* colours by its present owner, Rob Davies, the Mustang is a familiar participant at airshows and air events all over the UK.

UNITED STATES OF AMERICA
P-51A 43-6251 (N4235Y)
Planes of Fame Air Museum, Chino, California, USA

Built at North American's Inglewood factory, this particular early mark of Mustang saw no operational war service, instead it was used by a series of training units and the United States Army Air Force Technical School before being 'demobbed'. The fighter is reported to have had only 500 hours flying time on the airframe when it was grounded.

Planes of Fame Air Museum purchased the Mustang way back in 1953, but it remained in storage until early 1981, when a rebuild to flying condition was started. Fortunately, when the aircraft was dismantled for storage it was taken apart properly and all 'loose items' were bagged and put away for safe keeping. The aircraft was found to be in very good condition, which augured well for a speedy rebuild and in August 1981 the Allison-powered P-51A undertook its first post-restoration flight in the hands of Steve Hinton.

In the following month the Planes of Fame crew took the Mustang to Reno and competed in the annual Reno Air Races. N4235Y has been a regular participant at West Coast airshows ever since.

P-51D 44-13105 (N71FT) *Strega*
Bill Destefani, Shafter, California

This is one of several Mustangs in the USA, which have been highly modified for the spectacular sport of unlimited air racing (see Mustang Racers chapter). The annual Reno Air Races have been a regular haunt for *Strega* and

its supremely capable team of engineers — indeed, the aircraft regularly vies for first position 'past the post' with a glut of radial-engined Bearcats and Sea Furies, along with all the other Mustangs battling it out at this thrill-packed event.

Although originally built for the USAAF, this P-51 went to the Royal Australian Air Force as A68-679 in 1945 and served with the Australians until December 1948. In the 1960s it was displayed in a static condition in its A68-679 makings inside the Warbirds Aviation Museum at Mildura, Victoria, but during the early 1980s it was purchased by American warbird restorer and engine specialist David Zeuschel and shipped to Van Nuys, California.

Rebuilt to flying condition and modified solely for the purpose of unlimited air racing, the Mustang employed a number of special features, like a custom-built underbelly airscoop, a one-piece lowered cockpit canopy, Hoerner wingtips, plus a highly-tuned Merlin engine.

Given the name *Strega* (Italian for Witch) by its new owner, Bill *Tiger* Destefani, this P-51 is one of a special breed of warbird, the unlimited racer!

P-51D 44-73206 (NL3751D) *Hurry Home Honey*
Charles Osborn, Louisville, KY
One of the Mustangs which was 'demobbed' at McCellan AFB, California in 1958, was this fighter, registered as N7724C to Trans Florida Aviation at Sarasota, Florida in 1963. This tenure of ownership lasted three years and in 1966 it was re-registered to a new owner as N3751D. However, ten years later, the Mustang was resident in Tahiti and appeared on the French civil aircraft register as F-AZAG.

Owned during this period by Jean-François Lejeune, the fighter eventually returned to the USA in 1983 and was restored at Chino, emerging in the colours of *Hurry Home Honey*, and coded JF-L. Owned by Al Ashbourne and operated out of Chino, the Mustang was by now back on the American register as NL3751D, an identity that it retains to this day. Acquired by its present owner in 1985, modifications were made to the paint scheme, in that the Mustang now flies as '413586' C5-T, although it still retains its familiar nose art.

P-51D 44-74950 (NL51DT) *Slender, Tender & Tall*
Dick Thurman/Vintage Warbirds Inc, Louisville, KY
Little is known of this Mustang's service career, if indeed it actually had one! It appeared on the American civil reg-

ister as N5464V early in 1963 and later that year was sold on to Melvyn Paisley, who re-registered it as N511D. The aircraft crashed and was destroyed in August 1971, but by then it was being operated by the Mustang Pilots Club Inc at Van Nuys, California.

However, the power of the warbird rebuilders in the USA is not to be ignored and by 1976 the aircraft had re-emerged as N20JS and was operated by John Silberman at Key West, Florida. A change of ownership to Selby Burch in November 1984, prompted a register change to N7496W. The fighter was sold yet again in 1994, this time to Dick Thurman's Vintage Warbirds Inc at Louisville, Kentucky, and it continues to be flown in its 352nd Fighter Group colours and markings.

P-51D 44-74966 (N5410V) *Dago Red*
Museum of Flying, Santa Monica
Another of the famous Reno air racers, *Dago Red* is a composite airframe which was originally put together by Bill *Tiger* Destefani and Mike Nixon. The racing modifications were largely based on Mustang N79111 *Jeannie*, another successful racing aircraft. Little is known of its military career — assuming it had one — but the aircraft is known to have 'surfaced' in 1963 when it was registered as N5410V to the Prevost Smith Parachute Company at Santee, California.

After passing through a couple of private owners, the Mustang was acquired by *Tiger* Destefani who proceeded to modify the fighter for the sole purpose of unlimited air racing. The wingtips were clipped, the canopy reduced to a much lower profile and the airframe generally cleaned up to squeeze out extra miles per hour on the racing circuit. Mike Nixon worked on the Merlin engine, increasing its output dramatically and *Dago Red* was born!

This was a two-year process and in 1983 the fighter was registered to Frank Taylor Racing Inc at Bakersfield, California. Two more owners later, the Mustang is still a

regular participant at air events, in particular the annual Reno Air Races in Nevada.

F-6D 44-84786 (N51BS)

Henry J Schroeder, Danville, Illinois

Originally built at Dallas, Texas, as a P-51D, this example was subsequently modified to F-6D configuration, the photo reconnaissance variant and was delivered to the USAAF on June 8, 1945. Assigned to the 3rd Air Force, based at Key Field, Mississippi, it served with the 347th Base Unit.

The Mustang went on to fly with the 363rd Reconnaissance Squadron, 69th Tactical Reconnaissance Group at Brooks Field, Texas, and was later re-worked by Air Material Command at Pope AFB to RF-51D status in July 1946. March 1948 saw the fighter flown to McCellan AFB in California, where it was declared as surplus. According to Air Force records, the aircraft was 'scrapped' in November, but after a failed attempt to smuggle the Mustang to Israel it was sold to Mike Coutches, who subsequently put the RF-51D in his back yard where it was used as a plaything by his children!

In 1961 it was sold to Bill Myers of St Louis, Missouri, who started a long-term rebuild to flying condition. Little work was carried out on the airframe, and in 1981 the Mustang was acquired by its current owner. Seeing as the fighter was complete, Schroeder decided to restore it to stock condition and the aircraft was moved to Danville, Illinois. In the main, the work was carried out by the owner and a few volunteers, with specialist items being sent out to sub-contract agencies. Slowly but surely the fighter gained shape in what was to become one of the most precise P-51 restorations in history. After a ten-year rebuild the Mustang flew again on June 17, 1993, emerging from the hangar in a highly polished natural metal finish, complete with the codes 5M-K and *Li'l Margaret* emblazoned on the engine cowlings.

P-51D 45-11553 (NL51VF) *Shangri La*

Charles Osborn/Mustang Air Inc, Wilmington, DE

Although currently in the markings of Captain Don Gentile's *Shangri La,* this particular Mustang was previously flown under the guise of the chequerboard-nosed *Jacky C.* Sold as surplus at McCellan AFB, California in 1957, the aircraft was initially put onto the American civil aircraft register as N5414V, but was re-registered as N713DW when purchased by Richard Weaver at Van Nuys in 1963. Richard raced the Mustang as #6, which was later changed to #15. Ownership was subsequently transferred to Thomas Neal in 1970 and in 1972 Anthony D'Alessandris of Reno, Nevada, purchased the fighter and re-registered it as N22DC. During this owner's tenure the Mustang had its civil registration changed four times, ending up as N5415V.

The aircraft was rebuilt after an accident and ownership was taken on by Erin Rheinschild of Unlimited Air Racing Inc at Van Nuys. It again entered the racing arena, this time as #553 *Miss Fit.* After more damage, the Mustang was rebuilt by NA-50 Inc at Rialto, California, and put into the markings of the 78th Fighter Group's WZ-I *Jacky C,* flying for the first time in this new guise in June 1993. Currently operated by Charles Osborn, this example is a regular participant at American air displays and associated air events.

Cavalier Mustang II 67-22581 (N151MC) *American Beauty*

Max Chapman, Kissimmee, FL, USA

Trans-Florida Aviation Inc (which later became the Cavalier Aircraft Corporation) was responsible for the conversion and development of several versions of the F-51 Mustang for private executive and sport flying during the 1960s. *American Beauty,* formerly the well-known *What's Up Doc"* is one of those in question.

The prototype Cavalier conversion first flew in 1961 and featured a number of improvements to the basic Mustang airframe. A second seat was fitted behind the pilot's, which meant removing the standard radio gear and fuel tank. Baggage space was provided in a rear fuselage hold or in the old gun bays in the wings. The cockpit cabin and seats had de-luxe upholstery, with foam rubber seat cushions, and floor carpets. Soundproofing was also upgraded considerably, as were the heating and ventilation systems. In order to give better directional stability the new aircraft were fitted with a taller fin and rudder assembly.

C-GMUS was built by the Cavalier Aircraft Corporation in February 1968 and was taken on the strength of the Fuerza Aerea Boliviana (Bolivian Air Force) on May 9, 1968, as FAB 523. The aircraft served the Bolivians well for a decade and was eventually retired and traded for a batch of armed Lockheed T-33 Silver Stars in early 1968.

FAB 523 was purchased by a private owner in Canada who registered the airframe as C-GMUS and one year later was acquired by Ross Grady. The Edmonton-based Mustang retained its Bolivian colours and markings, and was a regular participant at air events all over Canada and the USA for many years.

Now owned by Max Chapman, *What's Up Doc* has forsaken its well-known colour scheme and appears on the air display circuit as *American Beauty.*

Below: Charles Osborn's P-51D *Shangri La* eases up to the cameraship during a photo sortie out of Oshkosh in 1997. (Key – Duncan Cubitt)

Bottom: With full flap deployed and the throttle being eased gently back, Cavalier Mustang II C-GMUS comes into land at Oshkosh in 1995. At this time the aircraft was still owned by Ross Grady and carried the familiar *What's Up Doc* markings. (Key – Duncan Cubitt)

Above: Three North American P-51D Mustangs formate for the camera of Duncan Cubitt during a sortie out of an EAA Oshkosh Fly-in. (Key – Duncan Cubitt)

Worldwide Mustang Survivors Directory

Of all the world's airworthy warbirds, the North American Mustang is the most numerous. It is believed that there are now over 150 flyable examples of the P-51 dotted around the globe, and a total of over 250 surviving airframes. Considering that the aircraft was conceived as long ago as 1940, these are incredible statistics! The numbers of airworthy Mustangs is increasing all the time as airframes are being rescued, restored and put back into the air.

This directory of the airframes which are flyable, on display in museums, and undergoing restoration to static or airworthy standard, has been compiled using a number of different sources and was as accurate as possible at the time of this book going to press. It does not include wrecks, 'paperwork' airframes or aircraft remains where identification has, so far, proved to be impossible. It goes without saying that with the world's population of the P-51 changing almost on a daily basis (indeed some 12 changes of status have been amended to aircraft in this following listing during its gestation period before the book went to press), so some anomalies may have inevitably crept into the information presented here.

Mark	Identity	Owner/Operator/Location	Markings
AIRWORTHY MUSTANG SURVIVORS			
A-36A	42-83731/N251A	Tom Friedkin/Lone Star Flight Museum, Houston, TX, USA	
P-51A	43-6006/N51Z	Jerry Gabe, San Jose, CA, USA	Polar Bear
P-51A	43-6251/N4235Y	Planes of Fame Air Museum, Chino, CA, USA	'AG470/RU-M'
P-51A	43-6274/N90358	Charles Nichols, Chino, CA, USA	'AX-H'
P-51C	42-103645/NL61429	CAF, St Paul, MN, USA	Tuskegee Airmen By Request
P-51C	42-103831/NX1204	Kermit Weeks, Miami, FL, USA	INA The MACON BELLE
P-51D	44-10753/NL405HC	Heber Costello estate, Oak Grove, CA, USA	It's About Time
P-51D	44-13016/NL5551D	Calvin Burgess, Bethany, OK, USA	Dove of Peace
P-51D	44-13105/N71FT	Bill Tiger Destefani, Shafter, CA, USA	Strega Race #7
P-51D	44-13250/N151DM	Dan Martin, San Jose, CA, USA	Ridge Runner III
P-51D	44-13257/N51DL	Ed Lindsay, Sarasota, FL, USA	
P-51D	44-15651/NX79111	Jimmy Leeward, Ocala, FL, USA	Leeward Ranch Special Race #9
P-51D	44-15757/N51WB	Wiley Sanders, Troy, AL, USA	Jeannie Too
P-51D	44-63350/NL51TK	Charles Greenhill, Kenosha, WS, USA	Lou IV
P-51D	44-63476/N63476	Bob May	City of Winnipeg
P-51D	44-63507/NL51EA	Swiss Warbirds, FMA, Altenrhein, Switzerland	Double Trouble Two
P-51D	44-63542/N51HR	Ted Contri, Carson City, NV, USA	Sizzlin' Liz
P-51D	44-63576/N51DH	Evergreen Vintage Aircraft Corp, McMinnville, OR, USA	
P-51D	44-63634/NL51ES	Ed Shipley, Malvern, PA, USA	Big Beautiful Doll
P-51D	44-63655/N5500S	AMBHIB Inc, Wheeling, IL, USA	Geraldine
P-51D	44-63663/NL41749	Richard Hansen, Batavia, IL, USA	Miss Marylin II
P-51D	44-63675/NL1751D	Roger Christgau, Eden Prarie, MN, USA	Sierra Sue
P-51D	44-63701/N26PW	Sal Rubino Jr, Merced, CA, USA	Grim Reaper
P-51D	44-63807/N20MS	Edward Stringfellow, Birmingham, AL, USA	Tiger Lily
P-51D	44-63810/N451BC	Joe Newsom, Cheraw, SC, USA	Angels Playmate
P-51D	44-63864/G-CBNM	The Fighter Collection, Duxford, UK	Twilight Tear
P-51D	44-63889/N4034S	Gary McCann, Stratford, ON, Canada	
P-51D	44-63893/N3333E	Wayne Rudd, Basalt, CO, USA	Dixie
P-51D	44-64005/N51CK	Charles Kemp, Jackson, MS, USA	Mary Mine
P-51D	44-64122/N339TH	Wes Stricker, Jefferson City, MO, USA	Kansas City Kitty
P-51D	44-72035/G-SIJJ	Peter Teichman, North Weald	Jumpin Jacques
P-51D	44-72051/NL68JR	Roland Fagen, Granite Falls, MN, USA	Sweet Revenge
P-51D	44-72086/N510JS	Joseph Scogna, Yardley, PA, USA	Baby Duck
P-51D	44-72145/NL51PT	Peter McManus, Baltimore, MD, USA	Petie 3rd
P-51D	44-72192/N5460V	California Warbirds, Hollister, CA, USA	Straw Boss 2
P-51D	44-72216/G-BIXL	Robs Lamplough, North Weald, UK	Miss Helen
P-51D	44-72339/NL251JC	Cavanaugh Flight Museum, Dallas, TX, USA	
P-51D	44-72438/N7551T	Bob Jepson, Kissimmee, FL, USA	Hell-er Bust
P-51D	44-72739/NL44727	Elmer Ward, Chino, CA, USA	Man O War
P-51D	44-72773/G-SUSY	Paul Morgan estate, Sywell, UK	Susy
P-51D	44-72777/NL151D	Steve Sehgetti, Vacaville, CA, USA	Sparkie
P-51D	44-72811/NX47R	Steve Converse, Shafter, CA, USA	Huntress III
P-51D	44-72826/NL51YS	Steve Collins, Atlanta, GA, USA	Old Boy

Mark	Identity	Owner/Operator/Location	Markings
		AIRWORTHY MUSTANG SURVIVORS	
P-51D	44-72902/N335	V A Bonzer, Los Angeles, CA, USA	*American Dreamer*
P-51D	44-72907/N41748	Duane Doyle, Castro Valley, CA, USA	*Red Dog XII*
P-51D	44-72922/NL93TF	Jim Shuttleworth, Huntingdon, IN, USA	*Scat VII* (crashed and destroyed February 21, 2003)
P-51D	44-72934/XB-HVL	Humberto Lobo, Monterey, Mexico	*Shangri-La*
P-51D	44-72942/N5427V	Anthony Buechler, Waukesha, WI, USA	*Petie 2nd*
P-51D	44-73029/NL51JB	Jim Beasley, Philadelphia, PA, USA	*Bald Eagle*
P-51D	44-73079/N151BL	Bill Dause, Lodi, CA, USA	
P-51D	44-73129/N51SL	Stu Eberhardt, Livermore, CA, USA	*Merlin's Magic*
P-51D	44-73140/NL314BG	Flying A Services, North Weald, UK	*Petie 2nd*
P-51D	44-73149/G-BTCD	Old Flying Machine Co, Duxford, UK	*Ferocious Frankie*
P-51D	44-73206/NL3751D	Charles Osborn, Sellersburg, IN, USA	*Hurry Home Honey*
P-51D	44-73210/CF-IKE	Ike Enns, Winnipeg, MB, Canada	*Miracle Maker*
P-51D	44-73264/N5428V	CAF – Regis Urschler, Bellevue, NE, USA	*Gunfighter*
P-51D	44-73275/NL119H	James Elkings, Salem, OR, USA	*Never Miss*
P-51D	44-73287/N951M	Michael George, Springfield, OR, USA	*Worry Bird*
P-51D	44-73339	Terry Tarditi, Lodi, CA, USA	
P-51D	44-73350/N33FF	Lee Maples, Vichy, MO, USA	*Archie*
P-51D	44-73415/NX551VC	Bob Button, Bakersfield, CA, USA	*VooDoo Race #5*
P-51D	44-73420/ZK-PLI	Alpine Deer Group/B Hore, Wanaka, New Zealand	*Miss Torque*
P-51D	44-73436/NL51KD	Brian Reynolds, Olympia, WA, USA	*American Beauty*
P-51D	44-73454/NL2051D	Richard Bjelland, Stockton, CA, USA	*This Is It!*
P-51D	44-73458/N4151D	William Hane, Mesa, AZ, USA	
P-51D	44-73463/N351D	Bob Baker, Alva, OK, USA	*Oklahoma Miss*
P-51D	44-73518/N6WJ	Don Whittington, Fort Lauderdale, FL, USA	*Precious Metal Race #38*
P-51D	44-73543/N151TP	Tom Patten, Nashville, TN, USA	*Sweetie Face*
P-51D	44-73656/NL2151D	Vlado Lenoch, La Grange, IL, USA	*Moonbeam McSwine*
P-51D	44-73693/N35FF	Bill Rheinschild, Chino, CA, USA	*Risky Business Race #45*
P-51D	44-73704/NL6861C	Lewis Shaw, Dallas, TX, USA	
P-51D	44-73751/N5444V	Ron Van Kregten, San Jose, CA, USA	
P-51D	44-73822/N51BS	Butch Schroeder, Danville, IL, USA	*Lil' Margaret*
P-51D	44-73843/N10601	Carl Payne/CAF, Midland, TX, USA	*Old Red Nose*
P-51D	44-73856/NL7TF	Tom Friedkin, Chino, CA, USA	*Susie*
P-51D	44-73871/N7098V	Mustang Air Inc, Wilmington, DE, USA	Stephanie
P-51D	44-73877/N167F	Anders Saether, Oslo, Norway	*Old Crow*
P-51D	44-73973/NL151DP	David Price, Santa Monica, CA, USA	*Cottonmouth*
P-51D	44-73990/N51TH	Tom Henley, Emelle, AL, USA	*Alabama Hammer Jammer*
P-51D	44-74009 /N51KB	Bill McGrath, Nantucket, MA, USA	*Kat Bird*
P-51D	44-74012/N6519D	James E Smith, Kalispell, MT, USA	
P-51D	44-74311/N151KM	Ken McBride, Hollister, CA, USA	*RCAF 577*
P-51D	44-74389/N64824	Art Vance, Sonoma, CA, USA	*Speedball Alice*
P-51D	44-74391/N351MX	Chris Woods, Carefree, AZ, USA	
P-51D	44-74404/N151RJ	R Odegard, Kindred, ND, USA	*Dazzling Donna*
P-51D	44-74417/N6327T	Richard James, Fennimore, WI, USA	*Donna-Mite*
P-51D	44-74423/N64CL	Clay Lacy, Van Nuys, CA, USA	*Miss Van Nuys Race #64*
P-51D	44-74425/N11T	Tom van de Meullen, Lelystad, Holland	*Damn Yankee*
P-51D	44-74427/F-AZSB	JCB Aviation, Montpellier, France	*Nooky Booky IV*
P-51D	44-74445/N4132A	Bill Hubbs, Pecos, TX, USA	*Sugar Booger*
P-51D	44-74446/N1451D	Robert Davis, Tipton, IN, USA	*Saturday Night Special*
P-51D	44-74453/NL751RB	Bob Baranaskas, Northport, NY, USA	*Glamorous Gal*
P-51D	44-74458/N351DM	David Marco, Jacksonville, FL, USA	*Sizzlin' Liz*
P-51D	44-74466/N10607	Harry Barr, Lincoln, NE, USA	*Barbara Jean*
P-51D	44-74469/N1251D	Classic American Aircraft, Chino, CA, USA	*Tally Ho Two*
P-51D	44—74474/N6341T	Jack Rousch, Livonia, MI, USA	*Old Crow*

Below: Tom Friedken's unique airworthy North American A-36 Apache made a very welcome appearance at the UK's Flying Legends Airshow in 2002, where it was the undoubted star of the display. (Key – Duncan Cubitt)

Below: San Jose-based Jerry Gabe operates this P-51A *Polar Bear,* which was captured on film at the Edwards Air Force Base Open Day in 1997. (Key – Dave Allport)

Above: P-51C 42-103645 (NL61429) was rebuilt to flying condition over a number of years by members of the Commemorative Air Force's South Minnesota Wing, based at Minneapolis. Now immaculately turned out, the fighter pays tribute to the famed 'Red Tails', the Mustang unit operated by the Tuskeegee Airmen, during World War Two. (Key – Steve Fletcher)

Left: It's hard to believe that this partially rebuilt fuselage became the superb flying example seen in the adjoining illustration. Transported on a trailer to the CAF's South Minnesota Wing's annual airshow at Minneapolis in 1995, the P-51C was put on static display to raise funds for the remainder of its restoration. (Key – Robert J Rudhall)

AIRWORTHY MUSTANG SURVIVORS

Mark	Identity	Owner/Operator/Location	Markings
P-51D	44-74494/N72FT	Hugh Bikle, Mountain View, CA, USA	Iron Ass
P-51D	44-74502/N351DT	Dick Thurman, Louisville, KY, USA	Kentucky Babe
P-51D	44-74506/F-AZJJ	Rene Bouverat/Air B Aviation, Marnaz,, France	Juliette
P-51D	44-74524/N151HR	H Reichert, Bismarck, ND, USA	Dakota Kid
P-51D	44-74543/N4543	Richard Vartanian, Shafter, CA, USA	
P-51D	44-74582/N51JT	J Thibodeau, Denver, CO, USA	Crusader
P-51D	44-74602/N3580	Jack Hovey, Ione, CA, USA	
P-51D	44-74739/N51RH	John Bagley, Rexburg, ID, USA	Ole' Yeller
P-51D	44-74813/N251KW	Ken Wagnon, Danville, IL, USA	Cripes a Mighty
P-51D	44-74829/ZK-TAF	Graeme Bethell, Auckland, New Zealand	Rudolph
P-51D	44-74865/N8677E	Gene Mallette, Blackfoot, ID, USA	My Sweet Mary Lou
P-51D	44-74878/N6306T	Tom Wood, Indianapolis, IN, USA	
P-51D	44-74908/N151BP	Bob Pond, Palm Springs, CA, USA	
P-51D	44-74910/N74920	Charles Nichols, Chino, CA, USA	Miss Judy
P-51D	44-74950/NL51DT	Tom Blair, Potomac, MD, USA	Slender, Tender & Tall
P-51D	44-74976/N651JM	Jeff Michael, Lexington, NC, USA	Obsession
P-51D	44-74977/N5448V	Christopher Gruys, Santa Fe, NM, USA	
P-51D	44-74996/N5410V	Terry Bland, Mojave, CA, USA	Dago Red/Race #4
P-51D	44-75007/N3451D	Paul Poberezny, Oshkosh, WI, USA	Paul I
P-51D	44-75009/N51TC	Ted Contri, Carson City, NV, USA	Rosalie
P-51D	44-84390/N2869D	Doug Driscoll, American Falls, ID, USA	Section Eight
P-51D	44-84658/N51TF	John Macquire, Santa Teresa, NM, USA	The Friendly Ghost
P-51D	44-84745/N851D	Stallion 51 Corp, Kissimmee, FL, USA	Crazy Horse
P-51D	44-84753/N251BP	Bernie Jackson, Minden, NV, USA	The Vorpel Sword
P-51D	44-84850/N850AH	Anderson Aviation, St Augustine, FL, USA	Su Su
P-51D	44-84860/N327DB	Daryl Bond, Chino, CA, USA	Lady Jo
P-51D	44-84864/N4223A	Mike Coutches, Hayward, CA, USA	
P-51D	44-84900/N51YZ	Bill Allmon, Las Vegas, NV, USA	NACA 127
P-51D	44-84933/N201F	John Mark, Oshkosh, WI, USA	
P-51D	44-84952/N210D	Charles Monthon, Wilmington, DE, USA	
P-51D	44-84961/N7715C	Steve Hinton, Chino, CA, USA	Wee Willy II
P-51D	45-11381/N551CB	Gary Honbarrier, High Point, NC, USA	Glamorous Glenn III
P-51D	45-11391/N51WT	Wally Sanders, Manassas Apt, VA, USA	Nervous Energy IV
P-51D	45-11471/N51UR	Bob Jepson, Kissimmee, FL, USA	Diamondback
P-51D	45-11507/N921	Kermit Weeks, Polk City, FL, USA	Cripes a Mighty 3rd
P-51D	45-11518/G-MSTG	Maurice Hammond, Hardwick, Suffolk, UK	Janie
P-51D	45-11525/N151AF	Bill Anders, Eastsound, WA, USA	Val Halla
P-51D	45-11526/VH-FST	Rob Poynton, Canning Bridge, Australia	The Flying Undertaker

AIRWORTHY MUSTANG SURVIVORS

Mark	Identity	Owner/Operator/Location	Markings
P-51D	45-11540/N151W	Jim Reed, Chesterton, IN, USA	*Excalibur*
P-51D	45-11553/N51VF	Blue Sky Aviation, Streetman, TX, USA	*Shangri-La*
P-51D	45-11558/NL514DK	DK Warbirds Inc, Las Vegas, NV, USA	
P-51D	45-11559/N51MX	Max Chapman, Kissimmee, FL, USA	*Mad Max*
P-51D	45-11582/N5441V	Ed Maloney, Chino, CA, USA	*Spam Can*
P-51D	45-11628/N151X	William Hane, Mesa, AZ, USA	*Ho Hun*
P-51D	45-11633/N151MW	Bob Jepson, Kissimmee, FL, USA	*Lady Alice*
P-51D	45-11636/N11636	Michael Bertz, Broomfield, CO, USA	*Stang Evil*
P-51K	44-12140/N119VF	Aadu Karemaa, San Diego, CA, USA	
P-51K	44-12840/N51EW	Valhalla Aviation Inc, Van Nuys, CA, USA	*Montana Miss*
P-51K	44-12852/N357FG	Jim Beasley Jr, Philadelphia, PA, USA	*Frenesi*
P-51H	44-64314/N551H	Mike Coutches, Hayward, CA, USA	
P-51H	44-64415/N49WB	Whittington Bros, Fort Lauderdale, FL, USA	
Cavalier II	67-22579/N251RM	Russ McDonald, Park City, UT, USA	*Newf*
Cavalier II	67-22580/N2580	Chuck Hall, Ramona, CA, USA	*Six Shooter*
Cavalier II	67-22581/N151MC	Max Chapman, Kissimmee, FL, USA	*American Beauty*
CA-17	A68-1/N51WB	Wiley Sanders, Troy, AL, USA	*Jeannie Too*
CA-17	A68-39/N551D	Jack Erickson, Medford, OR, USA	
CA-18	A68-100/N51AB	Brian Adams, Hollister, CA, USA	*Flying Dutchman*
CA-18	A68-104/VH-BOB	Bob Eastgate, Point Cook, VIC, Australia	
CA-18	A68-105/VH-JUC	Hourigan/Pay syndicate, Tyabb, VIC, Australia	
CA-18	A68-107/VH-AUB	Colin Pay, Scone, NSW, Australia	
CA-18	A68-110/VH-MFT	Warplanes Pty Ltd, Jindalee, QLD, Australia	*Snifter*
CA-18	A68-118/VH-AGJ	Jeff Trappett, Latyrobe Valley, VIC, Australia	*Eclat*
CA-18	A68-170/VH-SVU	RAAF Historic Flight, Point Cook, VIC, Australia	
CA-18	A68-175/NL64824	Art Vance, Santa Rosa, CA, USA	*Speedball Alice*
CA-18	A68-187/NL50FS	Frank Borman, Las Cruces, NM, USA	*Su Su II*
CA-18	A68-192/G-HAEC	Rob Davies, Woodchurch, Kent, UK	*Big Beautiful Doll*
CA-18	A68-198/NL286JB	Bill Bruggeman, Blaine, MN, USA	*Short-Fuse Sallee*

Above: 45-11525 (N151AF) *Val Halla* roars down the runway at the USAF's 50th Anniversary Airshow, held at Nellis AFB, Nevada, USA, in April 1997. (Key – Steve Fletcher)

Below: Jim Read's highly polished P-51D *Excalibur* takes off at Florida's Sun 'N Fun event in 1998. (Key – Duncan Cubitt)

Above: Colonel Regis Urschler's *Gunfighter* has been a regular performer at American air events for many years. Note the pilot's helmet wears the same chequerboard markings as does the fighter's nose! (Key – Duncan Cubitt)

Below: *Old Red Nose*, one of the Commemorative Air Force's founding aircraft (back in 1957 when the organisation was called the Confederate Air Force) is still going strong and is now operated on the CAF's behalf by Carl Payne. The Mustang, N10601, is based at CAF Headquarters, Midland, Texas, USA. (Key Collection)

Left: Eyeball to eyeball with a Mustang! The Old Flying Machine Company's P-51D 44-73149 (G-BTCD) is adorned with the markings carried by USAAF fighter pilot Wallace E Hopkins of the 374th Fighter Squadron, 361st Fighter Group, 8th Air Force. *Ferocious Frankie* nose-art compliments a colourful paint scheme. (Key – Duncan Cubitt)

Below left: *Su Su II* is an Australian-built Commonwealth Aircraft Corporation CA-18 Mustang A68-187 (NL50FS), which masquerades in a post-war TF-51 colour scheme. Based at Las Cruces, New Mexico, the aircraft is owned and flown by former Apollo astronaut Frank Borman. (Key – Duncan Cubitt)

Below: The UK's Flying Legends Airshow, organised by The Fighter Collection and the Imperial War Museum, and held annually at Duxford Airfield, always provides a spectacle of multiple Mustangs. Here, a quartet make their way out to the active runway in readiness for their display slot. Listen to those Merlins! (Key – Robert J Rudhall)

Left: The first Mustang to be operated in private hands in the UK was Charles Masefield's 44-74494 (N6356T), seen here at Shoreham Airport in May 1968. After winning the 1967 Kings Cup Air Race, the Mustang, painted in a smart red with white trim colour scheme, went on to appear at a number of air events before returning to the USA in 1971. The fighter still survives and is currently operated by Hugh Bikle, based at Mountain View, California. It currently wears military markings with the nose-art *Iron Ass* and is now registered as N72FT. (Stephen Reglar)

MUSEUM/DISPLAY			
Mark	**Identity**	**Owner/Operator/Location**	**Markings**
XP-51	41-038/N51NA	EAA Museum, Oshkosh, WI, USA	
A-36A	42-83665/N39502	USAF Museum, Dayton, OH, USA	*Margie H*
P-51D	44-13106/A68-648	RAAF Museum, Point Cook, VIC, Australia	
P-51D	44-13371	Hill AFB Museum, UT, USA	*Audrey*
P-51D	44-13571	Eglin AFB Museum, FL, USA	
P-51D	44-13704	Warner Robins AFB Museum, GA, USA	*Ferocious Frankie*
P-51D	44-14570	Barksdale AFB Museum, LA, USA	*Moonbeam McSwine*
P-51D	44-63615	Dover AFB Museum, DE, USA	*Bonnie*
P-51D	44-63871	Musee de l'Air, Paris, France	
P-51D	44-63992/Fv26020	Swedish Air Force Museum, Linkoping, Sweden	
P-51D	44-72123	Displayed on pole, Dominican Republic	
P-51D	44-72948	USAF Museum, Charlston, WV	*Wham Bam*
P-51D	44-72989	USAF Museum, Volk Field, WI, USA	
P-51D	44-72990/N6322T	USAF Museum, Fort Rucker, AL, USA	
P-51D	44-73347	National Aviation Museum, Ottawa, Canada	
P-51D	44-73349/J-2113	Swiss Air Force Museum, Dubendorf, Switzerland	
P-51D	44-73415	RAF Museum, Hendon, UK	*Little Friend*
P-51D	44-73444	Italian Air Force Museum, Vigna di Valle, Italy	
P-51D	44-73494	Seoul, Republic of Korea	
P-51D	44-73683	San Diego Aero Museum, San Diego, CA, USA	*Bunnie*
P-51D	44-73920	Chinese Military Museum, Beijing, China	
P-51D	44-73972	US Air National Guard Museum, Fresno, CA	
P-51D	44-73979	Imperial War Museum, London, UK	*Big Beautiful Doll*
P-51D	44-74216	USAF Museum, Tuskegee, Mobile, AL, USA	*Derailer*
P-51D	44-74229/F-362	Indonesian Air Force HQ, Jakarta, Indonesia	
P-51D	44-74407	USAF Museum, Heritage Park, ND, USA	
P-51D	44-74409/NL51RT	RAF Museum, Hendon, UK.	*Donald*
P-51D	44-74505/N68DR	Cuba	
P-51D	44-74827	RNZAF Museum, New Zealand	
P-51D	44-74939	NASM, Washington, DC, USA	*Willit Run?*
P-51D	45-11458/N4886V	Venezuala	FAB 504
P-51D	FAG 336	La Aurora AFB, Guatemala	
P-51D	IAF 303	displayed on pole, Halim, Indonesia	
P-51D	IAF 338	on display, Indonesia	
P-51D	IAF 347	on display, Indonesia	
P-51D	IAF 354	Palagan Museum, Ambarawa, Indonesia	
P-51D	IAF 363	on display, Indonesia	
P-51D	IDFAF 01	Israeli AF Museum, Hazor AFB, Israel	
P-51D	IDFAF 08	Israeli AF Museum, Hazor AFB, Israel	
P-51D	IDFAF 39	Israeli AF Museum, Hazor AFB, Israel	
P-51D	IDFAF 2338	Israeli AF Museum, Hazor AFB, Israel	
P-51K	44-12116/NX79161	F Crawford, Museum, Cleveland, OH, USA	*Second Fiddle*
P-51K	44-12125	RNAF Military Aviation Museum, The Netherlands	
P-51K	44-12458	PLA AF Museum, Datangsham, China	
P-51H	44-64265	Octoave Chanute Museum, Rantoul, IL, USA	
P-51H	44-64376	USAF Museum, Lackland AFB, TX, USA	
Cavalier II	68-15795	Air National Guard Museum, Minneapolis, MN, USA	

Below: The USAF Museum at Dayton, Ohio, USA, has a rare example of the North American A-36 Apache on display. 42-83665, *Margie H*, wears a standard olive drab colour scheme, but note the underwing bombs and deployed dive brakes. (Key Collection)

Above: Suspended from the ceiling of the Imperial War Museum's London, UK headquarters, P-51D 44-73979 wears the markings of the wartime Duxford-based 78th Fighter Group's Colonel John D Landers' *Big Beautiful Doll*. (Key – Duncan Cubitt)

Left: Displayed atop a substantial 'pole', Mustang F-363 graces the entrance of the Air Force Headquarters facility at Jakarta in Indonesia. (Key – Alan Warnes)

Left: The Royal Air Force Museum at Hendon, north London, UK, currently displays P-51D 44-73415 *Little Friend* in the Bomber Command Hall, as a tribute to the escort fighters of the USAAF. The aircraft is pictured here at RAF Halton, just after its arrival in the UK. However, with the recent donation of Robert C Tullis' P-51D '413317' (N51RT), it has been suggested that *Little Friend* may move northwards to the RAF Museum at Cosford. (Key – Dave Allport)

Right: Washington's National Air and Space Museum displays a P-51D, and quite rightly so. *Willit Run?* carries standard USAAF World War Two 8th Air Force markings and has been on show at the impressive museum for many years. (NASM)

Below: Looking a bit 'battered around the edges' and minus its tailwheel, Mustang 44-73920/'02' is nevertheless on public display at the Chinese Military Museum in Beijing, China. (Key – Alan Warnes)

Bottom: The Israeli Air Force Museum at Hatzerim has a number of Mustangs on display, of which the camouflaged '38' is one. (Key – Alan Warnes)

STORED/UNDERGOING RESTORATION			
Mark	Identity	Owner/Operator/Location	Markings
A-36A	42-83738/N4607V	John Paul, Caldwell, ID, USA	
XP-51G	43-43335	John Morgan, La Canada, CA, USA	Marjorie Hart
P-51A	43-6178/N51KW	Kermit Weeks, Polk City, FL, USA	
P-51B	43-12112	Ron Shirk, Plymouth, IN, USA	
P-51B	43-24760/NX28388	Mike Coutches, Hayward, CA, USA	
P-51C	43-25147/G-PSIC	The Fighter Collection, Duxford, UK	Princess Elizabeth
P-51C	44-10947/N1202	NASM, Washington DC, USA	Excalibur III
P-51D	44-11153/N451TB	Anthony Banta, Dover, DE, USA	
P-51D	44-13009/N31RK	Richard Knowlton, Portland, OR, USA	
P-51D	44-13278	Yugoslavia	
P-51D	44-13954	David Kingshott, Coventry, UK	Da Quake
P-51D	44-14574	Essex, UKLittle Zippie	
P-51D	44-63577/N151JT	John Turgyan, New Egypt, NJ, USA	
P-51D	44-63865/N151TF	Classic American Aircraft Inc, Poland, OH, USA	
P-51D	44-63889/N4034S	John D Anderson (under restoration with Sam Tabor, East Troy, Wisconsin, USA)	
P-51D	44-72028/G-LYNE	exported from UK to USA – Nov 2001	
P-51D	44-72059/N951HB	Vintage Aero, Wilmington, DE, USA	
P-51D	44-72202/ '325'	SAAF Museum, Lanseria, South Africa	Patsy Dawn
P-51D	44-72364/N723FH	Flying Heritage Collection, Rialto, CA, USA	
P-51D	44-72400	Woody Edmonson, Bradley, CT, USA	
P-51D	44-72936/N7711C	Marvin Crouch, Encino, CA, USA	
P-51D	44-73081/N5074K	Mike Coutches, Hayward, CA, USA	
P-51D	44-73098	Daytona Beach, FL, USA	
P-51D	44-73163/N51MR	Randall Kempf, Phoenix, AZ, USA	
P-51D	44-73254/N6328T	Don Weber, Baton Rouge, LA, USA	Buster
P-51D	44-73279	Bob Baker, OK, USA	
P-51D	44-73282/N151SQ	Square One Aviation, Chino, CA, USA	
P-51D	44-73323/N151MD	Marvin Crouch, Encino, CA, USA	
P-51D	44-73343/N5482V	Bruce Morehouse, Celeste, TX, USA	
P-51D	44-73574	Richard Ransopher, Kernersville, NC, USA	

Top right: This former Fuerza Aérea Guatemaltica P-51D 336 stands guard outside Aurora Air Force Base, Guatemala City. Despite being kept outside, the airframe looks to be in reasonable condition, although hopefully the cockpit canopy is closed when it rains! (Mario Flores Ponce)

Bottom: After suffering an accident during 2002, the South African Air Force Museum Historic Flight's P-51D 44-72202 Patsy Dawn was, at the time of this book's publication, being assessed to see if a restoration back to flying condition is viable. (Key – Tony Dixon)

Bottom: Obviously in need of much care and attention, this Mustang is one of those held by the Israeli Air Force Museum at Hatzerim. It may look as if it is beyond repair, but warbird restorers these days can work wonders, and have put far worse airframes back in the air. Who knows, this P-51 may well grace the skies once again in the future! (Key – Alan Warnes)

Above: As this book went to press The Fighter Collection's Duxford, UK-based P-51C 43-25147 (G-PSIC) *Princess Elizabeth* was approaching the end of a precise restoration programme and was expected to fly again in 2003. (Key – Nigel Price)

Overleaf: Pilot, and a very lucky passenger, get to sample the delights of flying the North American Mustang. Most of the preserved airworthy P-51s have the wartime radio equipment removed from behind the pilot and a 'jump' seat fitted so that two can 'share the magic'. (Key – Duncan Cubitt)

STORED/UNDERGOING RESTORATION

Mark	Identity	Owner/Operator/Location	Markings
P-51D	44-73902/N38227	Wilson C Edwards, Big Spring, TX, USA	
P-51D	44-74202/N5420V	Mike Coutches, Hayward, CA, USA	
P-51D	44-74204/N51U	K Shell	
P-51D	44-74230/N5466V	David Norland, Denver, CO, USA	
P-51D	44-74452/N74190	Wilson C Edwards, Big Spring, TX, USA	
P-51D	44-74483/N51GP	George Perez, Sonoma, CA, USA	*Race #8*
P-51D	44-74497/N6320T	Bob Jepson, Kissimmee, FL, USA	*Quicksilver*
P-51D	44-74536/N991R	Brent Hisey, Oklahoma City, OK, USA	*Miss America/Race #11*
P-51D	44-74797	Luis Villar, USA	
P-51D	44-74836	Brian O' Farrell, Miami, FL, USA	
P-51D	44-74923/N6395	Stichting Vroege Vogels, Lelystad, Holland	
P-51D	44-74962/N51DK	John Dilley, Fort Wayne, IN, USA	
P-51D	44-74978/N74978	Cal Pacific Airmotive, Salinas, CA, USA	
P-51D	44-75024/N96JM	John Macquire, Santa Teresa, NM, USA	
P-51D	44-84489/VH-AMG	Peter Anderson, Sydney, NSW, Australia	
P-51D	44-84615/N55JL	Jimmy Leeward, Ocala, FL, USA	*Cloud Dancer*
P-51D	*44-84847/N251RJ*	*James Maroney, Fargo, ND, USA*	
P-51D	44-84896/N5416V	Ken Scholz, Playa del Rey, CA, USA	
P-51D	44-84962/N9857P	Lee Schaller, New Athens, IL, USA	
P-51D	45-11439/N51HY	Hunter Barbara, Lewisburg, WV, USA	
P-51D	45-11513	John Smith, Mapua, New Zealand	
P-51D	44-73117/N251SQ	Square One Aviation, Chino, CA, USA	
P-51D/P-51XR	N6WJ	World Jet Inc, Fort Lauderdale, FL, USA	
P-51K	44-11807/N30991	Meryl Shawver, Mesa, AZ, USA	
P-51K	44-12118/N60752	Mark Tisler, Wahepeton, ND, USA	
P-51H	44-64375/N67149	James Parks, Bend, OR, USA	
Cavalier II	67-14866/N20TF	Tom Freidkin, Carlsbad, CA, USA	
CA-17	A68-71	Derek Macphail, Australia	

When World War Two came to a close, piston-engined fighters were rapidly retired as the more advanced jets came into service. It almost seemed as if the propeller fighter had seen its best times, when on June 25, 1950, the Communist North Korean Army crossed the 38th parallel into South Korea. It was this act of aggression, which would ultimately propel the North American Mustang back into combat. The Republic of Korea's military force was woefully inadequate to repel the Russian-supplied invaders and its army withdrew, somewhat in disarray. To its cost, the US rapidly discovered that it had insufficient troops based in Japan to carry out any realistic counter attack.

The bulk of the USAF's aircraft fleet was based in Japan which presented a major logistical problem. The USAF's 5th Air Force's commander, Lt Gen E Partridge realised that the only way of halting the rapid North Korean advance was to get as many USAF fighters into South Korea as quickly as possible. Every F-51 Mustang, which Partridge could get his hands on, was pulled out of storage and restored to combat readiness. Scraping up enough to equip one frontline fighter unit (a composite group known as 'Bout One'), the call then went out to the Air National Guard units in the USA for F-51s, which could be shipped out to South Korea. Thus the aircraft, which had already seen more than enough action in World War Two, found itself at the frontline of another conflict.

By the middle of July some 145 Mustangs has been gathered together and flown to Naval Air Station Alameda and made ready for shipping out to South Korea aboard USS Boxer. Accompanying the aircraft were 70 pilots, most of whom had served in Mustang units within the USAAF during World War Two. The famous fighter was back in the thick of it again!

At one time during the Korean War there were eight squadrons of operational Mustangs, including aircraft and units from the Royal Australian Air Force and the South African Air Force. Considering that it was really the age of the up-and-coming jet fighter (Sabre vs MiG), the North American piston-engined design acquitted itself extremely well. The portfolio of images in this chapter illustrate the varying colour schemes and conditions in which the F-51 Mustangs operated.

Above: Five Mustangs (wearing their trademark sharkmouths) of the 12th Fighter/Bomber Squadron are lined up at Seoul City Airport (K-16) in September 1951. This airport was a major staging post for a number of units from the Fifth Air Force. (B C Reed via Warren Thompson)

Below: The pilot, Captain Frank Buzze, and a member of the aircraft's groundcrew savour a moment of peace and quiet before the next 12th Fighter/Bomber Squadron sortie gets underway. Note that this Mustang sports drop tanks and a full complement of rockets. (Ed Nebinger via Warren Thompson)

Below: Australia was one of the first Commonwealth countries to join the United Nations in trying to stem the invasion of South Korea. Mustangs of the Royal Australian Air Force's 77 Squadron operated out of Iwakuni Air Base in Japan for some considerable time. They were later attached to the USAF's 35th Fighter Group and were based at Pohang. Strangely this is not an Australian-built Mustang, but a North American-constructed P-51D. (Bob Deward via Warren Thompson)

Left: F-51 Mustangs of the South African Air Force (SAAF) started operations in the Korean conflict during November 1950, after flying into their operating base at Pusan East Airfield. Nicknamed the Flying Cheetahs, the SAAF Mustangs were attached to the USAF's 18th Fighter Bomber Wing. SAAF pilots excelled themselves during the war and were awarded 55 Distinguished Flying Crosses. (Herb Pederson via Warren Thompson)

Left: Groundcrews worked tirelessly in order to minimise 'down time' on the Mustangs. In the early stages of the war facilities were rudimentary at some airfields, but as time passed improvements were made which enabled the aircraft to be serviced in reasonable conditions. The 18th Fighter/Bomber Wing's base at Chinhae was fortunate in that hangarage was available for major overhauls and deep servicing. Work can be seen taking place on these 39th Fighter Interception Squadron Mustangs during the autumn of 1951. (Glen Wold via Warren Thompson)

Left: Some of the first Mustangs to reach Korea, including those which served with 'Bout One', wore Republic of Korea Air Force markings, such as this example pictured in Japan during 1952. A number of these aircraft had previously been employed in target towing duties and were in less than perfect condition when they were pressed into operational service again. A heavy demand was placed on the aircraft of 'Bout One' and the unit shouldered the bulk of the flying operations until more F-51s arrived from the United States. (Bill Hastings via Warren Thompson)

Right: *Red Raider,* a Mustang on the strength of the 36th Fighter/ Bomber Squadron, 8th Fighter/Bomber Group, suffered damage after being hit by ground fire during a low level mission. One of the Mustang's major failings was that it was susceptible to small arms fire when employed on straffing operations. This aircraft, piloted by Ed Jones, fell foul of such retaliation and on landing swung off the runway into the mud. Two members of its groundcrew ponder how to get the aircraft back onto firmer ground using the recently arrived crane. (via Warren Thompson)

Right: Much use was made of napalm during the Korean War. This view shows Pusan Airfield, South Korea, operating base for the 40th Fighter Interception Squadron, 35th Fighter Group, in October 1950. The large number of napalm tanks in the foreground are being made ready for yet another air operation. (Duane Biteman via Warren Thompson)

Below: Major Bill Myers (right), wing maintenance chief of the 12th Fighter/Bomber Squadron, stands alongside an unidentified officer at Chinhae Air Base, South Korea. Parked behind them is one of the unit's distinctive sharkmouth-schemed Mustangs. (Bill Myers via Warren Thompson)

Above: Lt Duane Biteman, is pictured here, alongside Mustangs of the 12th Fighter/Bomber Squadron and 77 Squadron Royal Australian Air Force, both units of which operated out of Pusan Air Base. (Duane Biteman via Warren Thompson)

Above left: Aerial reconnaissance played a major role in the winning of the Korean War. Red-nosed Mustangs of the 45th Tactical Reconnaissance Squadron were very active and were equipped with standard F-51Ds and RF-51Ds. FF-735 *Mari Lou*, Fred Jones's aircraft of the 45th TRS, was one of the fighter versions of the Mustang which flew with the unit out of Taegu Air Base. (Fred Jones via Warren Thompson)

Left: Much of the routine servicing work took place in the open air during the Korean conflict. The ever-vigilant groundcrews can be seen here making minor repairs and getting the Mustangs ready for the next mission. (US National Archives)

Above: It was a classic case of 'improvisation in the field', as packing cases were used as workbenches and makeshift gantries were created for access to the engines of the Mustangs during the Korean War. (US National Archives)

Left: Merlin engines 'turning and burning', these F-51 Mustangs of the 18th Fighter Bomber Wing start to taxi out for take off on another operational sortie. (US National Archives)

This F-51D served with the 12th Fighter Squadron, 18th Fighter Bomber Group, based at Chinhae, South Korea during 1951. (Pete West)

⑨ MUSTANG RACERS

With so many combat aircraft surplus to requirements at the end of World War Two, it was a foregone conclusion that some of the fighter types from that conflict would find their way into private ownership and be used for recreational purposes. The prospect of entering Mustangs and the like in air racing competitions would, in time, bring a whole new meaning to the term 'unlimited' in racing circles.

The first post-war US National Air Race event was held at Cleveland, Ohio, in the autumn of 1946. The entire contingents for the Bendix Trophy Race and the Thompson Trophy Race were made up entirely of war surplus fighters. With all the military-style equipment stripped out by their owners, plus heavily boosted engines, Mustangs (along with a host of other World War Two fighter types for that matter) soon began to appear with special racing modifications. Cut-down cockpit canopies, clipped wingtips, highly polished airframes and probably the most important of all, wet wings. The latter feature comprised a wing structure, which was sealed and used to house the aircraft's fuel. This idea has now become commonplace on warbirds, which are used for air racing, but it actually originated with Major Alexander P de Seversky of the Republic Aircraft Company prior to World War Two.

The present-day American air racing scene is synonymous with Reno, Nevada, and each September large crowds gather at Reno-Stead Airport, a few miles outside the famed gambling city, to watch an aerial event which cannot be equalled anywhere else in the world. Some aviation historians argue that the major modifications, which take place on the participating aircraft, destroys their historical significance. Others appreciate the quest for speed and the dedicated work carried out by engineers, pilots and all the support crews which collectively provides the National Championship Air Races with the ultimate piston-engined warbird spectacle. Apart from the myriad of alterations made to the aircraft themselves, the advent of racing warbirds has often brought forth some smart, colourful, and sometimes downright outlandish, paint schemes.

Below: Summing up the colourful razzmatazz that pervades the air at Reno, Race #4, *Dago Red*, N5410V, taxies out from the pits in readiness for the afternoon's big race. Operated by the Santa Monica Museum of Flying, *Dago Red* has been a regular Reno attendee since it took the 'race circuit' by storm in 1982. (Key – Duncan Cubitt)

Right: Race City! A small village assembles at Reno each September as the aircraft and their extensive support teams descend on the Nevada airfield for the annual bout of high-powered excitement. Four Mustangs can be seen in this view of the 'pits' area, where the high-powered contenders are made ready for the challenge ahead. (Key – Duncan Cubitt)

Middle: Whenever Art Vance's P-51D NL64824 *Million Dollar Baby* attends the Reno Air Races, it comes accompanied by a novel means of crew transport. The motorised Mustang drop tank, seen here being driven towards the pits area, bears the legend *Half Million Dollar Baby*. (Key – Duncan Cubitt)

Bottom: Race #84 *Stilleto* was originally developed for unlimited air racing by Alan Preston. Built from scratch, with the aid of computer technology, by David Zeuschel at Slymar, California, using major parts of P-51D 45-11471, it featured cropped wings, deletion of the normal Mustang underbelly air intake and flush radiators in the wing leading edges. It won the Unlimited Gold Race in 1984 and when its days as a racer were over was restored back to TF-51 configuration. Now registered as N51UR it is operated by Bob Jepson and is based at Kissimmee, Florida. (Key – Duncan Cubitt)

Left: With 007 emblazoned on the fin and rudder (shades of James Bond!), Bill *Tiger* Destefani's *Strega* (N71FT) won the 1997 Unlimited Gold Race at a blistering 453.130mph. Featuring a custom-built airscoop, lengthened tailplane, turtledeck rear fuselage and modified cockpit canopy, the racer is seen here screaming around the pylons at Reno in 1994. (Key – Duncan Cubitt)

Below: *Miss America* has attended air races for many years. In terms of airframe modifications it is basically 'stock', but has featured Hoerner wingtips and different style cockpit canopies. Originally flown by newspaper magnate Howie Keefe, the P-51D (44-74536/N991R) is now operated by Brent Hisey and is based at Oklahoma City, OK, USA. It suffered an accident at the 2002 Reno meeting and at the time of this book going to press was in the process of being restored to flying condition again. (Key – Duncan Cubitt)

Right: Not all the racing P-51s feature heavy modifications. 44-72777 (NL151D) *Sparky,* operated by Steve Seghetti, retains its stock military configuration, with only its red nose adding a splash of colour to its USAAF military markings. (Key – Duncan Cubitt)

Right: The all-yellow Mustang 44-74739 (N51RH) was used for many years by Robert A *Bob* Hoover as the official 'race start' aircraft. The race competitors would all form up on Bob's P-51 and when all were in line he would lead them down the first straight, pull up from the lead position and declare "Gentlemen, you have a race". Hoover operated this particular aircraft for many years on the race and airshow circuit, becoming well known for his polished aerobatic routines in this and a Rockwell Shrike Commander. (Key – Duncan Cubitt)

Right: The pits area at Reno is always a hive of industry, with work continuously taking place on the various team's precious charges. It is not unknown for the ground support teams to be present with a number of large trailers, inside which everything is needed to tend to the needs of the aircraft. Even several spare engines are held in readiness, should they be required. It is not unknown for an aircraft to fly to Reno with a stock engine fitted, only to have it changed for a specially 'souped up' racing engine in time for the races. After the races have finished the stock engine is refitted and the aircraft flies home! Here, *Strega's* Merlin engine is the centre of attention. (Key – Duncan Cubitt)

Left: *Cloud Dancer*, 44-84615 (NL55JL) has been part of the race circuit for many years, operated by Jimmy Leeward of the Leeward Air Ranch based at Ocala in Florida. Fitted with a Mike Nixon racing Merlin, 'Dancer also features clipped wings, with Hoerner wingtips. It is pictured coming in to land at Reno in 2000. (Key – Duncan Cubitt)

Centre: Two of *Dago Red's* groundcrew indulge in an informal post-race debrief with pilot Skip Holm. This view shows to advantage the aircraft's modified turtledeck rear fuselage and the small cockpit canopy. The paint scheme's pretty impressive too! (Key – Duncan Cubitt)

Bottom: Amid the typical Nevada landscape, one can almost feel the power of the Merlin as Skip Holm runs *Dago Red's* engine up prior to participating in the 1994 Unlimited Gold Race at Reno. The sound made by these aero engines, operating at high power settings during the races, has to be heard to be believed. The aircraft howl around the course making an almost ghostly sound quite unlike that heard during normal airshow demonstrations. (Key – Robert J Rudhall)

Right: Spectacular, but ill-fated! P-51D NX57LR *Miss Ashley II,* which was fitted with a modified LearJet wing, and powered by a Rolls Royce Griffon engine, driving contra-rotating propellers (shades of *The Red Baron*) made its Reno debut in the hands of Gary Levitz in 1997. This revolutionary aircraft was to meet a tragic end, when on September 18, 1999, it broke up in mid-air after suffering a catastrophic airframe failure, during the first lap of the Unlimited Gold Race. The aircraft fell out of the sky, killing 61 year-old pilot Levitz. It was the first fatality during an Unlimited race in the event's 36-year history. (Key Collection)

Below: Much-modified and re-engined with a Rolls Royce Griffon engine driving a contra-rotating propeller unit, P-51 Mustang N6WJ *Precious Metal* is without doubt an impressive piece of kit! Originally converted for unlimited air racing by Don and Bill Whittington of Fort Lauderdale, Florida. The aircraft is now owned by Ron Bucarelli, who intends to put the aircraft back on the racing circuit, but for one year only. Compared to the contra-rotating prop arrangement, the Griffon engine looks comparatively small in the airframe! (David Stephens Collection)

RED BARON – THE ULTIMATE RACING MUSTANG

By far the most famous of the racing Mustangs was N7715C. Built at Dallas, Texas, USA, as 44-84961, it was accepted by the USAAF on June 27, 1945. After spending a couple of years in storage at Kelly Air Force Base, Texas, it subsequently served with a series of Air National Guard units until it was retired and stored at McClellan AFB, Sacramento, California. Two years later it was put up for disposal and sold to Capitol Airways Inc, for the princely sum of $1,701, and entered onto the US Civil Aircraft Register as N7715C.

Five years later a three-man syndicate (Charles Hall, Frank Lynott and Charles Willis) purchased the Mustang for $7,735 and operated it until 1967, when Charles Hall became the sole owner. After making a number of structural alterations to the airframe and modifications to the engine the P-51 was entered in a series of air races sporting the legend *Miss R J* on the nose. In 1971 the aircraft was sold to Kalamazoo, Michigan-based Gunther Balz, who further modified the former fighter, naming the Mustang *Roto-Finish*, after his corporation.

Eventually, after passing through a couple more owners, the P-51 ended up in the hands of businessman Ed Browning. During 1974/75 the airframe was altered, yet again, with the intention of making it the world's fastest unlimited racing aircraft in the world. It emerged from a radical modification programme in June 1975, sporting a new and spectacular guise as the *Red Baron*. Sponsored by Red Baron Flying Services, which was based at Idaho Falls, Idaho, the company's engineers had performed miracles with this airframe. Gone was the familiar Merlin and in its place was a Rolls Royce Griffon 57, which had been taken from a British Avro Shackleton maritime patrol aircraft. The Shackleton's four engines were fitted with six-blade contra-rotating propellers, and this feature was carried over into the *Red Baron's* new persona. Now designated RB-51 the contra-rotating propeller feature eliminated any torque from the engine and prop unit. This proved to be of great benefit within the aircraft's flight envelope, even at low power settings.

During the late 1970s the *Red Baron* reigned supreme in the air racing stakes, with victory after victory. Initially piloted by Roy Mac McClain, from 1978 onwards the 'Baron flew in the hands of Steve Hinton, a young, but very experienced warbird pilot, and it was Hinton who had the World Speed Record in his sights. At that time the speed record was held by Darryl Greenamyer, who had piloted the much modified Grumman F8F Bearcat N1111L Conquest I at a blistering 483 mph over Edwards Air Force Base on August 16, 1969, thus breaking German Fritz Wendel's 1939 record in the Messerschmitt 109R (Me 209 V1).

Now, ten years later, Hinton and the *Red Baron* stood ready for a crack at the record. The team gathered at Tonopah Mud Flats, Nevada, in August 1979 and practice runs were plagued with a series of problems, which meant that an engine change would be required before any record attempt could be made.

Replacing the Griffon in just one day, a task which would normally have taken four days, the engineers worked through the night on August 10 to have the aircraft ready for the following morning. August 11 consisted of a day-long series of test flights, which apart from a few minor snags were satisfactory. Sunday August 12 dawned and the team were geared up ready to roll! *The Red Baron* took off, with Steve Hinton at the controls, and made four runs over the prescribed course. With the mighty Griffon churning out 3,200rpm the final run was hand-timed at 488mph. When the aircraft landed Hinton and the rest of the *Red Baron* team were confident that they had smashed the previous world record by a good margin. After the officials had viewed the film taken of the attempt they declared that the Mustang had been flying at 489mph for the last two runs over the course and that the *Red Baron* team now held the world speed record for a piston-engined aircraft. A triumph indeed!

Not content with this, two days later *The Red Baron* was airborne again trying to break its own record. An amazing 499mph was clocked on this occasion and Hinton had broken his own newly established record.

Four weeks later *The Red Baron* was to meet its demise, almost killing Steve Hinton in the process. During that year's Reno Air Races Hinton was piloting the Mustang around the pylons, when the Griffon suddenly failed. With the contra-rotating propellers stuck in an un-feathered position, acting as massive airbrakes, the aircraft rapidly fell out of the sky and smashed into the ground. As the fighter slid along the Reno scrubland one wing was torn off, the engine broke away from the fuselage and the aircraft finally came to rest in pieces. It was nothing short of a miracle that the cockpit area had more or less stayed intact and Steve Hinton was still alive. He was rushed to hospital with multiple injuries and after an amazingly short time in intensive care was seeing visitors just a few days later.

Today the *Red Baron* is no more, but Steve Hinton and his father-in-law, Ed Maloney (owner of the Planes of Fame Air Museum at Chino) acquired the paperwork identity for N7715C from Ed Browning. Using a multitude of parts from other airframes, including major portions of a former Indonesian Air Force P-51D, the rejuvenated N7715C flew again for the first time after rebuild in August 1984, with its new owner at the controls, none other than Steve Hinton!

To participate in warbird air racing one has to be prepared to spend large amounts of money! Any serious competitor needs to be aware that their hands have to plunge deep into the wallet. The initial purchase cost of acquiring a suitable Mustang (Bearcat, Sea Fury, or anything of this ilk) is likely to be in the region of $1.5 million, and that's if one can be found for sale. To prepare it for racing another $500,000 is needed for the many airframe and engine modifications if the aircraft is to have a fighting chance.

Finally, any owner needs to allow for the average of $2,000 required for every hour the aircraft flies and just in case an engine blows up and a replacement has to be found, an extra $150,000 needs to be put aside. That said, there is nothing to compare with the incredible sight and sound of these former weapons of war fighting it out at high speeds around the pylons at Reno. It is an experience that, once sampled, is never forgotten!

Left Looking smart in its civilian paint scheme, N7715C sits on the ramp at Reno in 1966. Who would have thought that in a little over ten years time this Mustang would be transformed into the dramatic speed-blistering machine known as the *Red Baron!* (Dick Phillips collection)

Right: Flying as *Miss R J* the Mustang sported a number of racing modifications: streamlined airframe, Hoerner wingtips and cut-down cockpit canopy. Note the extra-pointed propeller spinner in this 1973 view. (Dave Ostrowski via Dick Phillips)

Centre right: By 1973, *Miss R J* had changed owners and been re-christened *Roto-Finish*. Structurally the airframe remained unaltered. The most dramatic re-incarnation of this aircraft was yet to come!

Below: The ultimate racing Mustang, the *Red Baron*. Gone is the Merlin engine, replaced by a mighty Griffon (which produced between 3,400 and 4,000hp), driving a pair of contra-rotating propeller units. To help cope with this immense increase in power the fin and rudder area was considerably enlarged. When this photograph was taken the 'Baron held the record for the World's Fastest Piston-Powered Aircraft. Sadly, it was all to end on September 16, 1979, when the aircraft was totally destroyed in a crash at Reno. (William T Larkins via Dick Phillips)

MUSTANG FIELDS

Within this book's space constraints is impossible to enumerate every single airfield/airstrip used by the P-51 Mustang during its long and very successful military career, there are simply far too many! Therefore, in this brief overview of 'Mustang Fields' we feature a random selection of airfields used by the P-51s of the famed US 8th Air Force and the Royal Air Force in the UK during World War Two.

In the early period of the Mustang's use in the UK the fighter operated mainly from all-grass airfields (as fighters had done from the start of the war in most theatres of operation), but the weather in Great Britain was, and still is, unpredictable, to say the least. This led to many airfields being put out of action, or having restricted use, due to waterloging. Indeed, the Americans nicknamed Duxford Airfield (home to the 78th Fighter Group) 'Duckpond' due to the large number of occasions that rain had made the airfield unsuitable for operations to be mounted.

Pierced Steel Planking (PSP) became a temporary, but effective, answer for the inclement weather problem, and the laying of PSP 'runways' allowed the majority of sorties to be mounted, giving the airfields a better all-round operational capability. As the war progressed hard runways were laid, considerably improving the situation.

Above: Although this World War Two view of Honington shows a good number of B-17 Flying Fortresses dotted around the hangars, the base was home to the Mustangs of the 364th Fighter Group, comprising the 383rd, 384th and 385th Fighter Squadrons. The 364th FG also operated Lockheed P-38J Lightnings, the 'famed fork-tailed devil'. (Russel J Zorn)

Left: Now the headquarters of the Royal Air Force Regiment, Honington is now much changed from its wartime vista, and was last occupied by RAF Tornados of 13 Squadron RAF before being handed over to its present incumbents. (Key – Ken Delve)

Bottom: Honington was the last UK of the 8th Air Force-occupied UK airfields to be handed back to the RAF after World War Two had ended. This ceremony took place in early 1946. In 1944 the base was in full swing and the pilot's room, pictured here in April, was fully kitted out with the squadron regalia of the period. (US National Archives)

Right: Duxford Airfield, or 'Duckpond' as the Americans called it, was home to the black and white chequerboard-marked P-51 Mustangs of the 78th Fighter Group. Dating back to World War One, Duxford has witnessed many famous comings and goings in the world of aviation. In 1938 it was home to the world's first operational Spitfire unit (19 Squadron) and Douglas Bader's famed Big Wing during the Battle of Britain in 1940. Post-war, RAF Hunters and Javelins flew from a new hard runway, the late 1960s saw it being used as a major location for the film epic *Battle of Britain,* and today it is a Mecca for historic aircraft preservation in Europe. Home to the Imperial War Museum's large collection of aircraft, a significant number of airworthy warbirds also operate from the site with organisations such as the Aircraft Restoration Company, B-17 Preservation, Old Flying Machine Company and The Fighter Collection, to name just a few. (Key – Malcolm English)

Right: Fowlmere was a satellite airfield for Duxford during the war, with Spitfires being dispersed there during the Battle of Britain period. Later in the war it was home to the 339th Fighter Group, which operated P-51B, C, D and K variants. (Key – Ken Delve)

Right: Wormingford, near Colchester, was originally built to accommodate a USAAF heavy bomber unit, but was instead allocated for fighter use. P-47 Thunderbolts of the USAAF 9th Air Force were the first aircraft to move in, but in April 1944 Mustangs of the 55th Fighter Group, 8th Air Force took up residency. In 2002 the outline of the intersecting runways could still be seen and much of the airfield's surviving perimeter track was still being used by farmers. (Key – Ken Delve)

Left: Raydon Airfield, near Ipswich, was another location originally to be used by bombers, although when the bomber units were re-assigned to the 15th Air Force in Italy Raydon was occupied by fighters. Major user of the base was the 353rd Fighter Group, initially equipped with the P-47 Thunderbolt, but converting to the P-51 in October 1944. The 353rd flew some 447 operational missions during its time at Raydon, claiming an amazing 330 1/2 enemy aircraft kills in the air, plus 414 destroyed on the ground. This view shows construction of one of Raydon's T2 hangars underway by the 833rd Engineer Battalion in 1942. (US National Archives)

Left: Maurice Hammond's beautifully restored P-51D, 45-11518/G-MSTG Janie, wears the colours of the Raydon-based 353rd FG. The fighter is pictured parked on the grass at the 2001 Raydon Wings Airshow. This was an historic day, as it was the first time since the end of World War Two that a Mustang painted in the markings of the 353rd FG had operated out of the airfield! (Key – Steve Fletcher)

Left: Military airfields during World War Two became small communities in their own right and recreational needs for those housed on base had to be provided for. At Raydon, Duffy's Tavern, 'Where the elite meet to eat', was a popular haunt for the airmen, as was the camp cinema/theatre. This 1944 view reveals that the Bob Hope comedy film *The Princess and the Pirate* was being shown at a 13.30 matinee. (US National Archives)

Right: Little Walden Airfield was built in 1943 and the following year was occupied by Douglas A-20 Havocs of the 409th Bomb Group. However, in September of '44 it was handed over to the 8th Air Force, which immediately transferred the Mustang-equipped 361st Fighter Group from its less than ideal base at Bottisham. The 8th AF left the airfield in November 1945 and it was then used as a military vehicle store until final closure in May 1958. Now returned to farmland, several of the airfield buildings, including the control tower, remain standing and in use. (Key – Ken Delve)

Right: North Weald Airfield in Essex was occupied by Mustangs of the RAF's 2 Squadron, before the unit was deployed overseas during the war. Post-war it was home to the RAF's famous 111 Sqn aerobatic team, The Black Arrows, and in more recent years has become a haven for privately owned historic aircraft, ranging from DH Tiger Moths to Hawker Hunters. It is also the location for the annual fly-in organised by The Squadron in conjunction with *FlyPast Magazine*. This aerial view was taken during the 1997 *FlyPast Fly-in* and shows a wide variety of aircraft types on the ground. (Key – Robert J Rudhall)

Right: Although the RAF's 19 Squadron will always be remembered for ushering in the Supermarine Spitfire into military service, from 1944 to 1946 the unit operated Mustang IIIs and Mustang IVs. One of the airfields used by the 2 Sqn during this time was Southend in Essex. In recent years Southend Airport has been mainly used for general aviation, business and charter flights, along with airliner maintenance. This view, taken in 2002, shows a disparate collection of aircraft, including the Vulcan Restoration Trust's Avro Vulcan B.2 XL426 (G-VJ.ET), which is lovingly maintained in taxiable condition. (Key – Ken Delve)

Left: Steeple Morden was originally built as a satellite airfield for Bassingbourn, some three miles to the north-east. The P-47-equipped 355th Fighter Group took up occupancy in July 1943, converting to the Mustang in March 1944. This unit became the 8th AF's most successful ground-straffing fighter group, destroying 502 enemy aircraft on the ground. Returned to the RAF at the end of World War Two, Steeple Morden was closed down in September 1946. (Key – Mark Nicholls)

Left: Although little evidence of Steeple Morden's wartime activities survives, this impressive memorial is dedicated to the 355th FG. In addition to the Mustang propeller unit, crests for the 354th, 357th and 358th Fighter Squadrons, the 355th Fighter Group and the 2nd Air Division are also displayed. (Key – Duncan Cubitt)

Left: Mustang IIIs of the RAF's 118 Sqn operated out of Bentwaters Airfield in early 1945, before moving out to Fairwood Common. Post-war Bentwaters was used by the USAF, flying F-86 Sabres, TB-26 Invaders, F-101 Voodoos, F-4 Phantoms, A-10 Thunderbolt IIs and F-16 Fighting Falcons, during which time many improvements were made to the airfield and its infrastructure. The Americans moved out in 1993 and the airfield was used for the final time by RAF Harriers on exercise in September 1994. Today, Bentwaters is unused and bears little resemblance to its wartime vista. (Key – Ken Delve)

Right: Biggin Hill will always be associated with RAF Fighter Command's struggle against the Luftwaffe in the summer of 1940. However, in 1945 Mustang IVs of the RAF's 154 Sqn occupied the famed Battle of Britain station. Still very active today, 'Biggin on the bump' is a thriving general aviation and business airfield, the annual Biggin Hill International Air Fair (Britain's longest-running privately-organised airshow) giving visitors to the airfield a chance to see some of the aircraft types which operated out of the airfield during the dark days of World War Two. It is a foregone conclusion that most of these airshows will have featured either a Spitfire or Mustang! (BAE SYSTEMS)

Centre: Sadly, today not much of the historic Martlesham Heath Airfield survives. One-time home to the Aeroplane and Armament Experimental Establishment, between April and June 1941 Hurricane IIs of the American-manned RAF 71 (Eagle) flew from the airfield. This was indeed a portent of things to come, when in October 1943 P-47 Thunderbolts of the 356th FG, 8th Air Force, arrived. In November 1944 this unit re-equipped with the P-51 Mustang. Unfortunately the Group suffered the highest loss rate proportional to enemy aircraft destroyed of all fighter units in the 8th Air Force. When the Americans moved in hard runways were laid, with Pierced Steel Planking (PSP) being used in large amounts to create perimeter track taxiways. This diagram shows Martlesham Heath in its wartime configuration, with the hard runways and taxiways being represented in black, while the PSP taxiways and fighter dispersal's are shown in grey. (Key – Mark Nicholls)

Right: Mustangs of No's 2, 4, 63, 168, 170, 239, 268 and 400 Squadrons, RAF, all operated out of Odiham at varying stages of World War Two. These days this large airfield, with its long runway and plentiful hardstandings, is inhabited by RAF helicopters. No's 7, 18 and 27 Sqns operate the twin-rotor Boeing Chinook, while 657 Sqn flies the Westland Lynx. (Key – Ken Delve)

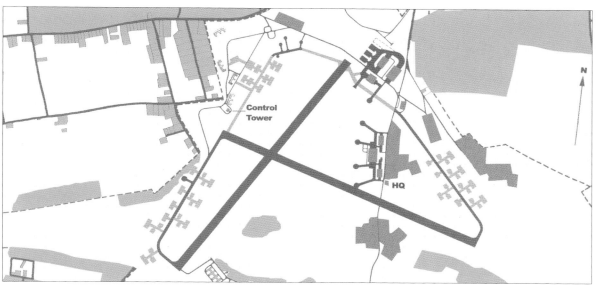

Bathed in the setting Florida sun, TF-51 Mustang *Crazy Horse*, operated by the Stallion 51 Corp, flies for the camera of Duncan Cubitt. One can almost hear the Rolls Royce Merlin engine roaring away. (Key – Duncan Cubitt)